SOME LANDMARKS OF TWENTIETH CENTURY CONTRACT LAW

SOME LANDMARKS OF TWENTIETH CENTURY CONTRACT LAW

SIR GUENTER TREITEL

Oxford · Clarendon Press

*This book has been printed digitally and produced in a standard specification
in order to ensure its continuing availability*

OXFORD
UNIVERSITY PRESS

Great Clarendon Street, Oxford OX2 6DP

Oxford University Press is a department of.the University of Oxford.
It furthers the University's objective of excellence in research, scholarship,
and education by publishing worldwide in

Oxford New York

Auckland   Cape Town Dar es Salaam   Hong Kong   Karachi
Kuala Lumpur Madrid Melbourne Mexico City Nairobi
New Delhi Shanghai Taipei Toronto
With offices in
Argentina Austria Brazil Chile Czech Republic France Greece
Guatemala Hungary Italy Japan South Korea Poland Portugal
Singapore Switzerland Thailand Turkey Ukraine Vietnam

Oxford is a registered trade mark of Oxford University Press
in the UK and in certain other countries

Published in the United States
by Oxford University Press Inc., New York

ISBN 978-0-19-925575-7

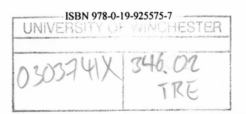

Preface

This book is based on the Clarendon Lectures in Law given in Oxford in October 2001. The text as reprinted retains its original lecturing style, though I cannot pretend that it was possible to deliver the whole of that text in only three lectures.

The main debt here to be acknowledged is that which I owe to the English judiciary and (it is to be assumed) indirectly to the bar. Without their sublety, inventiveness, and ingenuity, the work of a commentator on English contract law could not have continued to fascinate me, as it has done, for more than forty years. It is a reflection of this point that my concern in these lectures has been almost exclusively with judicial developments of the subject; and any doubts that I may occasionally have ventured to express about the reasoning in some of the cases should not be allowed to obscure, or be taken to derogate from, the debt that I owe to these sources.

On a more personal level, my thanks are due to Professor Peter Birks QC, not only for having invited me to give these lectures long after the age of my compulsory retirement, but also (and yet more warmly) for his unfailing kindness and constant encouragement at times when the task seemed to be, and perhaps was, beyond me. I am most grateful, too, to the publishers for having undertaken the task of getting an old-fashioned manuscript typed, for their help in many other ways, and for their hospitality.

Oxford   G.H.T.
December 2001

Contents

Table of Cases

Table of Cases

Table of Legislation

STATUTORY INSTRUMENTS

Introduction:
Scope of Discussion

It is about five and a half years ago since I last lectured in this room. At the end of that lecture I said that I had just given my last lecture on contract in Oxford and no doubt that statement gave considerable satisfaction to the exiguous audience present on the last Friday morning of Hilary Term 1996. If only a member of that audience who had acted in reliance on that statement were here today, it would be at least arguable that I was estopped from continuing with this series of lectures; but I rather fear that those of you who are here today are either too young or too old or too discriminating to have been here on that occasion. So I am bound by my promise, made to Peter Birks about four years ago, when he kindly offered to take me out of mothballs, to go on.

Since then, I have become more and more aware of the difficulties of performing that promise. One source of difficulty is that, during those four years, lectures in this series have been given by speakers whose distinction, wisdom, and scholarship I cannot hope to match. Another difficulty or group of difficulties is self-inflicted and lies in the subject that I chose—'Some Landmarks of Twentieth Century Contract Law'. For one thing, I knew that I should be criticized for looking back when the fashion is to look forward: surely, I should be expected to talk about contract law in the twenty-first century. But this is one (perhaps the only) point on which I believe myself to be on firm ground. If I imagine a contract lawyer of a hundred years ago trying to anticipate what lay ahead, I very much doubt whether he could have foreseen even the outcome of the coronation cases, the first of which lay only a few months ahead,[1] and in another

---

[1] The earliest reported coronation case appears to be that of the decision of Darling J in *Krell v Henry* given on 11 August 1902, just two days after the postponed coronation: see The Times, 12 August 1902; (1902) 18 TLR 823; the decision was affirmed on appeal [1903] 2 KB 740, by which time the defendant's counterclaim for the return of his advance payment had been withdrawn.

of which—*Chandler v Webster*[2]—a mistake was made which it took the courts[3] and Parliament[4] about forty years to put right, let alone the many other legal developments of the new century. In the present world of even faster change, it would be little short of science fiction to try to forecast what lies ahead.

For another, there is the problem of choice. When I think of my hypothetical contract lawyer of a hundred years ago, I cannot repress a tinge of envy. Let me assume that he would, like me, have chosen to look back on the previous century. How easy it would have been for him to choose his topics! My hypothetical friend would surely have lectured on *Hadley v Baxendale*,[5] on *Taylor v Caldwell*,[6] and (I rather think) on *Hochster v de la Tour*,[7] though I should not have regarded him as wholly eccentric if he had instead chosen *Carlill v Carbolic Smoke Ball*[8] or some of the cases that I shall have to mention by way of background to my twentieth century landmarks; or, if his interest had been in legislative techniques, he could have talked about the so-called codification of the law relating to bills of exchange, partnership, and sale of goods.

Today the choice is much more difficult. I am not good at counting words or cases, but no one needs such statistics to realize that the rate at which new material now comes from the courts and is reported (or available though unreported) hugely exceeds that of a hundred years ago—a fact reflected in the Lord Chief Justice's recent Practice Direction on the citation of authorities in court.[9] The analysis of this phenomenon could be the subject of another course of lectures; and its existence increases the difficulty of choice. This is made yet more severe by the problem of what may be called territorial scope. It is, for instance, quite strongly arguable that some of the most important landmarks in twentieth century contract law were the American Law

---

[2] [1904] 1 KB 493.

[3] *Fibrosa Spolka Akcyjna v Fairbairn, Lawson, Combe Barbour Ltd* [1943] AC 32.

[4] Law Reform (Frustrated Contracts) Act 1943, s 1(2).

[5] (1854) 9 Ex 341.   [6] (1863) 3 B & S 826.

[7] (1853) 2 E & B 67.   [8] [1893] 1 QB 256.

[9] Practice Direction of 9 April 2001, [2001] 1 WLR 1001.

Institute's Restatement of Contracts, the Uniform Commercial Code (especially Articles 1 and 2), and the incorporation of that Code's innovations into the Restatement, Second. But such a global approach, even if limited to common law jurisdictions, would make an unwieldy subject wholly unmanageable. My main focus will therefore be on the English law of contract, though some reference to authorities from other jurisdictions will have to be made where they have affected developments here.

Even the restriction to developments in England leaves a further problem. The growth in secondary sources has scarcely lagged behind the growth in case law and legislation: there has been a considerable increase in the number of contract textbooks, of monographs on many aspects of contract law, and of periodical literature of many kinds. But for most of the twentieth century the secondary sources had little influence in the courts, though in the last quarter, or more particularly in the last decade, of the century things began to change in this regard, perhaps because an increasing proportion of the judiciary and the bar had read law in the universities—a trend that imposes new and awesome responsibilities on those of us who teach, or write about, the subject here. Academic contribution to legislation affecting the subject has also been by no means negligible through membership of, and help given to, various law-reforming bodies. But most academic work continues to be by way of reaction to primary sources, and it is with these that I shall be mainly concerned. There is also the point that, in trying to assess the significance of secondary sources, I could scarcely hope to be even-handed.

Even with this restriction, the choice of topics that can be covered in three lectures must to a considerable extent be arbitrary (a sort of legal *Desert Island Discs*) though I hope that my choice is not entirely eccentric. So far as time allows, I shall deal with three topics. The first is the renegotiation (or variation) of contracts, where the centre-pieces will be the *High Trees*[10] case and *Williams v Roffey*

---

[10] *Central London Property Trust Ltd v High Trees House Ltd* [1947] KB 130.

Brothers.[11] The second is the battle over privity: here the discussion will revolve around the *Midland Silicones* case[12] and *Beswick v Beswick*.[13] And the third is the distinction between various types of contractual terms: the main focus of attention here will be the *Hong Kong Fir* case.[14] No doubt to many of you all this will be familiar ground: like Mark Antony, 'I tell you that which you yourselves do know.'

Before moving on to these topics, I should refer briefly to the great non-event of the period: we have escaped codification. The first item in the first programme of law reform issued by the Law Commission in 1965 was a recommendation 'that the law of contract be examined with a view to codification'.[15] Notice the caution with which the recommendation was framed: it was not a proposal *to codify* the law of contract, but a proposal that it should be *'examined with a view to codification'*—a distinction that came to receive some emphasis when the proposal later ran into difficulties. Many of these difficulties stem from a serious underestimate of the complexities of the task. One of the reasons given in 1965 in support of the codification proposal was that 'the general principles of the law of contract are now well established and the Commission regards it as ripe for codification'.[16] It seems that the two parts of this (in retrospect surprising) statement were intended to be linked: in other words, that it meant 'well established' and *therefore* 'ripe for codification'. But even in 1965 the general principles of contract law were by no means as 'well established' as the Law Commission's statement asserts; and there is reason to suppose that the assertion was at least in part based on accounts of the subject which failed to give due prominence to its many areas of obscurity, uncertainty, and controversy. And, if the Law Commission's statement was

---

[11] *Williams v Roffey Bros & Nicholls (Contractors) Ltd* [1991] 1 QB 1.
[12] *Scruttons Ltd v Midland Silicones Ltd* [1962] AC 446.
[13] *Beswick v Beswick* [1968] AC 58.
[14] *Hong Kong Fir Shipping Co v Kawasaki Kisen Kaisha Ltd* [1962] 2 QB 26.
[15] First Programme of the Law Commission (1965) Part I.
[16] Ibid.

questionable when it was made, developments in the next few years were to cast still further doubts on its validity. Those years saw a series of decisions of the House of Lords each of which marked a significant change in such important parts of the subject as exemption clauses,[17] damages,[18] third party beneficiaries,[19] and mistake.[20] There were equally important developments in the lower courts; and the remaining decades of the twentieth century saw an acceleration of the process of ever increasing sophistication and refinement in the field of contract law. These developments not only show that the Commission was on treacherous ground in its 'ripe for codification' statement. They also raise the question whether codification, had it occurred, would not have inhibited some of these developments which have, on the whole, improved the law, though they have certainly increased its complexity. One of the Commission's other reasons for embarking on the codification project was that the 'clarity and accessibility' of the law of contract were 'of greatest importance' as this branch of the law was the 'basis of trading and many other relationships'.[21] The difficulty with this part of the reasoning is that 'clarity' in a code may well imply a degree of rigidity; and as Sir Michael Kerr (who was to become the third Chairman of the Law Commission soon after the events to be related below) was later to say, when he had become Kerr LJ: an 'unfortunate effect of codification is that such terms [ie the terms of a codifying Act] become incapable of natural development. They become set in concrete.'[22] So codification might (I do not put it more strongly than that) have impeded some of the later judicial developments. Some of these, particularly those which relate to failure to perform

---

[17] The *Suisse Atlantique* case [1967] 1 AC 361 p 128 *post*.

[18] *Koufos v C Czarnikow Ltd (The Heron II)* [1969] AC 350.

[19] *Beswick v Beswick* [1968] AC 58 p82 *post*.

[20] *Gallie v Lee* [1971] AC 1004.

[21] First Programme of the Law Commission (1965) Part I.

[22] *State Trading Corporation of India Ltd v M Golodetz Ltd* [1989] 2 Lloyd's Rep 277, 289. The reference is to the Marine Insurance Act 1906 as interpreted by the Court of Appeal in *The Good Luck* [1989] 2 Lloyd's Rep 550; that decision was reversed on appeal: [1992] 1 AC 283 p 127 *post*.

stipulations as to the time of performance,[23] have also served to promote one of the Commission's objectives (that of 'clarity'[24]) as well; though this can scarcely be said of other judicial developments. To illustrate the latter point, one need refer only to decisions on such topics as the common law of restraint of trade[25] and damages in respect of a third party's loss.[26] All these judicial developments were, on the whole, beneficial and the fact that they were made casts doubt on the assertion that, before they occurred, the law of contract was 'ripe for codification', as well as on the view that codification was a desirable goal.

At an early stage of its work on the proposed Contract Code, the Commission took two decisions which greatly increased the difficulty of the project. The first was 'to reform as well as to codify';[27] the second was to produce a Code which 'will, so far as possible, be common to both England and Scotland'[28]—'and one which will in due course facilitate a closer association between the United Kingdom and the Continent of Europe'.[29] The last point reappears in the following year when we find a reference to 'the importance of achieving harmonisation with continental systems, the relevance of which has been enhanced by the Government's application to join the Common Market'.[30] In the later work on the Code, this objective of 'harmonisation with continental systems' was not pursued with as much vigour as the objective of harmonization with Scots law, perhaps because Scots law was at least ascertainable while, by contrast, 'continental systems' exhibited considerable variety *inter se*; work on a uniform European Contract Law still lay in the future. But though the objectives of combining codification with reform and of producing a Code for the whole of Great Britain were pursued

---

[23] *Bunge Corporation v Tradax Export SA* [1981] 1 WLR 711; *Union Eagle Ltd v Golden Achievement Ltd* [1997] AC 514 p 120 *post.*   [24] *Supra*, at n 21.

[25] *Esso Petroleum Co Ltd v Harper's Garage (Stourport) Ltd* [1968] AC 269.

[26] *Alfred McAlpine Construction Ltd v Panatown Ltd* [2001] 1 AC 518.

[27] Law Commission, *First Annual Report* §31 (1966).   [28] Ibid, §32.

[29] Ibid.

[30] Law Commission, *Second Annual Report* §29 (1967).

with considerable energy, they gave rise to two obvious and very considerable problems. The first was that of identifying defects in and divergences between the two constituent systems; and the second that of agreeing on common solutions. The resulting tension, particularly that resulting from important differences of basic principle between the English and the Scots law of contract, is diplomatically reflected in the Law Commission's Third Annual Report in 1968: 'Since both Commissions and their advisers are conscious of the defects as well as the merits of their own systems and are rapidly being educated in the defects and merits of the other, we are hopeful that it will prove possible to suggest solutions which are an improvement on both.'[31] An admitted preference for the ills we have might have been more realistic.

In spite of all these difficulties, a text of what the Law Commission's Seventh Annual Report (1972) described as 'preliminary drafts intended to lay the foundations of a Contract Code'[32] was completed, thanks largely to the energy and skill of Mr Harvey McGregor (now Dr Harvey McGregor QC). In using the phrase 'preliminary drafts', the Law Commission pointed to the next stage of the process: 'we have been working closely with the draftsman [that is, with Parliamentary Counsel] who has the task of putting the Commission's proposals into a form appropriate for legislation'.[33] The 'preliminary drafts' lacked the precision and detail commonly found in Acts of Parliament: they were regarded more as statements of legislative policy than as the implementation of such policy in statutory language. The task of translating (the term is not too strong) from the one medium or language into the other proved difficult in the extreme. A small part of the task came close to being accomplished in draft statutory provisions relating to contract formation; but the complexity of the task made

---

[31] Law Commission, *Third Annual Report* §9 (1968).
[32] Law Commission, *Seventh Annual Report* §7 (1972). The text is reprinted in McGregor, *Contract Code Drawn up on behalf of the English Law Commission* (Milan, 1993).
[33] Law Commission, *Seventh Annual Report* §7 (1972).

progress slow and time-consuming. The enthusiasm for a Code applicable to both England and Scotland had also waned. The Law Commission's Seventh Annual Report tells us that 'it will be for consideration at a later stage whether or not it is practicable to have a Contract Code for the whole of Great Britain'.[34] Soon afterwards, the Scottish Law Commission withdrew from the project[35] and this, together with the difficulty of what I have called the process of translating the 'preliminary drafts' into statutory language, led the Law Commission in 1973 to announce that it had 'suspended' work on the Contract Code project.[36] The completion of that project was regarded, not as impossible, but as too labour-intensive to be worth while: 'Several years' work would probably be needed before we were in a position to publish a contract code for England alone';[37] and the benefits that might be derived from such a Code, which were at best speculative, were not considered to be sufficient to justify the effort. In modern jargon, the exercise was not cost-effective; and the Commission turned instead to the task (which is still in progress) of reforming particular areas of contract law.

In retrospect, that decision seems to have been a sound one. Codification of contract law faces a dilemma. In common law countries that have codes of or including contract law (such as India and the Field Code States in the United States) the vague language of the relevant codes has done little, if anything, to improve the 'clarity and accessibility'[38] of contract law which were the Law Commission's declared aims in launching the project. A more precise and detailed Code along the lines envisaged in the Law Commission's Seventh Annual Report in 1972[39] might have helped to promote these objectives, but only (in all probability) at the expense of an unacceptable degree of rigidity. On balance, my conclusion is that the decision to 'suspend' the process was indeed a fortunate one and that

---

[34] Law Commission, *Seventh Annual Report* §7 (1972).
[35] See Law Commission, *Eighth Annual Report* §3 (1973).
[36] Ibid, §4.   [37] Ibid, §3.
[38] *Supra*, at n 21.   [39] *Supra*, at n 33.

development by judicial activity, and, where appropriate,[40] by legislation reforming specific parts of the subject, has proved to be the preferable option.

[40] As in the field of the law of third party beneficiaries: see pp 101–102 *post*.

1

Agreements to Vary Contracts

1. INTRODUCTION

The legal problems that I am going to discuss under this heading are of very considerable antiquity. They go back at least to Roman law, where we are told that a bare pact does not give rise (or birth) to an obligation but does give rise to a defence;[1] and where pacts varying a contract are consequently divided into those which diminish and those which increase an obligation,[2] some legal effect being given to the former but not to the latter. I shall not venture into that territory except perhaps to wonder why the Roman lawyers did not (so far as I know) ever have recourse to the metaphor of a bare pact being available as a shield but not as a sword;[3] and to say that similar problems have troubled English lawyers and have been the subject of considerable development in the twentieth century. The legal problems to which 'pacts' which vary contracts give rise have, in English law, been analysed in terms of 'consideration' and 'estoppel'; the respective spheres of operation of these doctrines has been, and remains, a source of controversy. Underlying the debate is the traditional definition of 'consideration' as a detriment to the promisee or a benefit to the promisor;[4] and there are cross-currents of public policy, duress, and unconscionability. To see where we stood at the beginning of the twentieth century, we shall have to look at some well-known nineteenth century cases. One part of the topic will take us on a journey from *Stilk v*

---

[1] Dig 2. 14. 7. 4.   [2] Dig 18. 1. 72. pr.
[3] This formerly 'time honoured phrase' (*Syros Shipping Co SA v Elaghill Trading Co (The Proodos C)* [1980] 2 Lloyd's Rep 390, 391) has now sunk to the level of a 'misleading aphorism' (*Baird Textile Holdings Ltd v Marks & Spencer plc* [2001] CLC 999, [2001] EWCA Civ 274, [52]).
[4] See eg *Currie v Misa* (1875) 1 LR 10 Ex 153, 162.

Myrick[5] to *Williams v Roffey Bros*;[6] the other from *Foakes v Beer*[7] to the *High Trees*[8] case—and (in each case) beyond. This division corresponds with the Roman distinction between increasing and decreasing pacts, though the English cases do not make the same use of it as the Roman sources do.

2. INCREASING PACTS

(a) Consideration, Public Policy, and Duress

Stilk v Myrick was the well-known case in which two members of the crew of a British ship had deserted in a Baltic port and the captain promised the other nine to divide the wages of the two between them if replacements could not be found, as turned out to be the case. The claim of the nine to enforce this promise was dismissed, according to one report,[9] because they had provided no consideration for the captain's promise, according to the other because enforcement would be contrary to public policy.[10] If we ask what is the underlying public policy, the answer is that enforcement might promote what we should now call economic duress, a category not then recognized by law. That argument may have been persuasive in the earlier case of *Harris v Watson*[11] where a considerable extra amount (5 guineas) was promised while the ship was in danger at sea 'to induce the seamen to exert themselves'; but it was much less so in *Stilk v Myrick* where the ship was safely in port when the captain's promise of extra pay was made, and it seems that even the further prosecution of the voyage was not directly imperilled. This accounts for the fact that Lord Ellenborough looked for a rationale different from 'public policy' and the one he found was lack of

---

5 (1809) 2 Camp 317; 6 Esp 129.
6 *Williams v Roffey Bros & Nicholls (Contractors) Ltd* [1991] 1 QB 1.
7 (1884) 9 App Cas 605.
8 *Central London Property Trust Ltd v High Trees House Ltd* [1947] KB 130.
9 2 Camp 317.   10 6 Esp 129.   11 (1791) Peake 102.

consideration. The sailors had provided no consideration for the captain's promise of extra pay because they were already 'bound by the terms of their original contract to exert themselves to the utmost to bring the ship home'. In other words the crew provided no consideration because they suffered no detriment. The question whether the captain got any benefit as a result of the crew's response to his promise was simply not discussed; and this lacuna in the reasoning provided scope for twentieth century development.

Both the strands of reasoning in these early cases reappear in twentieth century cases, though the public policy argument now appears under the heading of economic duress and slightly, but significantly, changes its shape. A modern example to illustrate these points is provided by *Atlas Express v Kafco* (1989)[12] where the defendants were suppliers of basketware to Woolworths and the plaintiffs were carriers who had contracted with the defendants for the carriage of their goods to Woolworths. The plaintiffs then demanded higher charges than those originally agreed and the defendants reluctantly agreed to pay them because it was very difficult or impossible for them to make alternative carriage arrangements to meet their agreed delivery dates with Woolworths. The carriers' claim for the extra charges was dismissed for two reasons. The first was that there was no consideration for the defendants' promise to pay the extra charges since 'the plaintiffs were already obliged to deliver the defendants' goods at the rates agreed under the original agreement'.[13] This was exactly Lord Ellenborough's 'consideration' reasoning in *Stilk v Myrick*. The second was that the defendants' promise had been procured by economic duress, an argument not open to the courts in the old cases on seamen's wages since the concept of economic duress did not surface in English law until 1976.[14] The argument in the *Atlas Express* case was that the

---

[12] *Atlas Express Ltd v Kafco (Importers and Distributors Ltd)* [1989] QB 833.
[13] Ibid 841.
[14] *The Occidental Worldwide Investment Co v Skibs A/S (The Siboen and The Sibotre)* [1976] 1 Lloyd's Rep 293, 335.

defendants had no real choice: there was no other way in which they could perform their contract with Woolworths in time, and they were a small company whose success depended on their being able to perform that contract. This may look like the old public policy argument in the cases on seamen's wages but there is a significant difference. The public policy argument could be, and apparently was, based on *hypothetical* duress: if the sailors could recover the extra pay, then they *might* refuse to perform their contracts. The modern economic duress argument will work only in cases of *actual* duress. It is also narrower in scope than the 'lack of consideration' reasoning of the old cases: that is, it invalidates fewer promises if only a way can be found to satisfy the consideration requirement. There are two reasons why it is narrower. First, we have the authority of *Pao On v Lau Yiu Long*[15] for saying that it is not every threat to break a contract which amounts to duress. In that case, the risk of loss likely to result from carrying out a threat of this kind was small so that the threat had little (if any) coercive effect and the threat was therefore held not to amount to duress. Secondly, there is the even more obvious point that there will be no duress if nothing is threatened at all. In the old cases on seamen's wages, there is nothing in the reports to indicate that any threats were made: even in *Harris v Watson* (where the ship was in danger when the promise was made) the threat was the imagined one that the men 'would *in many* cases suffer a ship to sink unless the captain would pay any *extravagant* demand they *might* think proper to make'. Were they really about to take to the boats? The doctrine of consideration may, in these old renegotiation cases, have sometimes operated as a sort of surrogate for an imperfectly developed law of duress; but it was a less than satisfactory surrogate, or too blunt an instrument, because the nature of the consideration reasoning was such that it could make a promise invalid even though no pressure had been exerted by the promisee at all. This defect was to some extent remedied by restrictions on the

---

[15] [1980] AC 614; cf *Huyton SA v Peter Cremer GmbH* [1999] 1 Lloyd's Rep 620.

scope of the consideration requirement in the renegotiation context, restrictions which were inherent in its original formulation. The requirement was satisfied if the promisee did *more* than he was originally required to do under his contract with the promisor[16] or if he was *discharged* from that contract, eg by supervening events, and then made a fresh promise to perform what he had been obliged to do under that discharged contract.[17] But if supervening events (or the discovery of antecedent circumstances) did *not* discharge the contract, this way of evading the consideration requirement was apparently not open, even though a renegotiation after such an event (or discovery) might make perfectly good commercial sense. The American case of *Watkins v Carrig*[18] (relevant to our discussion because of references to it in the English cases[19]) was of this kind. The contract was to excavate a cellar at a fixed unit price; after the work had begun it was unexpectedly discovered that about two-thirds of the materials to be excavated consisted of hard rock and the parties agreed that a substantially higher unit price (nine times the originally agreed amount) should be paid for doing this part of the work. The contractor's argument that the contract was voidable for mistake was rejected, even though the American doctrine of mistake is considerably wider than the corresponding English doctrine; but the contractor's claim for the extra payment was nevertheless upheld. The reasoning was that the site-owner had made a gift to the contractor of his (the owner's) right to have the work done for the originally agreed price; and, having in this way got rid of the original obligation, the court found no difficulty in holding that there was consideration for the subsequent promise. This reasoning has not attracted the English courts; their difficulty was probably with its first limb. So the case has had a hostile reception here; there are dicta to the effect that it would not

---

[16] eg *Hanson v Royden* (1867) LR 3 CP 47; *North Ocean Shipping Co v Hyundai Construction Co Ltd (The Atlantic Baron)* [1979] QB 705.

[17] eg *Liston v SS Carpathian (Owners)* [1915] 2 KB 42.

[18] 21 A 2d 591 (1941).

[19] *The Atlantic Baron* (n 16 supra) 714; *Williams v Roffey Bros* (n 6 supra) 21.

be followed in England.[20] If the contractor had in good faith believed that the original contract was invalid for mistake or had been discharged by frustration, it might be arguable that the subsequent agreement satisfied the requirement of consideration: that might follow from an analogous extension of the rule that a compromise of a disputed claim is binding, even though the claim was bad in law, if it was honestly and reasonably believed to be valid.[21] But such reasoning would not apply in the absence of any such belief. That may seem to be unfortunate: I am not arguing that the contractor should be entitled to extra pay in the absence of a renegotiation, but if the parties agree to change the terms in the light of unexpected events or discoveries, why should that agreement not be enforced? The most obvious answer is that it was procured by duress and there is perhaps a hint of this in *Watkins v Carrig*: the contractor had threatened to walk off the job. But if an argument of duress was put, it did not impress the New Hampshire court: 'Conceding that the plaintiff threatened to break its contract because it found the contract to be improvident, yet the defendant yielded to the threat without protest, excusing the plaintiff, and making a new arrangement'.[22] Perhaps there was no duress as the plaintiff's will was not overborne.[23] But it is also arguable that what may be called a whiff of duress is another reason for the hostile reception of the case in England.

(b) Three-Party and Public Duty Cases: Benefit to Promisor

Meanwhile, there was a cross-current which was, I believe, to have considerable influence on the renegotiation problem even though the cases in question were not concerned with renegotiation of an earlier contract between promisor and promisee. They raised instead the questions whether the promisee provided consideration by performing or

---

[20] See n 19 *supra*.

[21] *Callisher v Bischoffsheim* (1870) LR 5 QB 449.   [22] 21 A 2d 591, 594.

[23] For the present status of this line of reasoning in English law, see *Dimskal Shipping Co SA v International Transport Workers' Federation (The Evia Luck) (No 2)* [1992] AC 152, 166.

promising to perform a contractual duty which he owed to a third party. In the nineteenth century cases[24] there was some conflict and perhaps confusion on these issues, probably because of the difficulty in seeing what detriment was suffered by the promisee in such situations. But two late twentieth century cases decide both questions in favour of the promisee, *The Eurymedon*,[25] holding that *performance* of a contractual duty owed to a third party amounted to consideration because it benefited the promisor,[26] and *Pao On v Lau Yiu Long*,[27] that the same was true of a *promise to perform* such a duty. One possible ground for distinguishing these cases from the two-party cases is that there is 'less likelihood of economic coercion'[28] in the three-party than in the two-party cases. But this is not wholly convincing, especially where (as in the *Pao On* case) the promisee's prior contractual duty is owed to a company in which the promisor is a substantial shareholder. The argument that the promisor had been subjected to economic duress was, indeed, rejected in that case, but the rejection was *not* based on the fact that the promisee's original duty was owed to the company rather than to the shareholders; it was instead based on the fact that the promisee's threat to break their contract with the company did not have sufficient coercive effect on the promisor. So far as the requirement of consideration was concerned, this was satisfied because the promisor benefited from the new arrangement in that it increased the likelihood that the promisee's duty to the company would be performed.

This element of benefit to the promisor also appears in the cases in which consideration has been held to consist in the performance of a so-called 'public duty', that is, a duty imposed by law rather than by contract. Benefit to the promisor is expressly made the ground of decision on the

---

[24] eg *Shadwell v Shadwell* (1860) 9 CB (NS) 159; *Jones v Waite* (1839) 5 Bing NC 341, 351 (affirmed on another ground (1842) 9 Cl & F 107).
[25] *New Zealand Shipping Co Ltd v AM Satterthwaite & Co Ltd (The Eurymedon)* [1975] AC 154.
[26] Ibid 168 ('for the benefit of the shipper').   [27] [1980] AC 614.
[28] Restatement, Contracts, 2d §73 Comment *d*.

consideration point by Denning LJ in two such cases: *Ward v Byham*[29] and *Williams v Williams*;[30] and, though he was alone in expressing that view in those cases, there are other recent indications[31] of the courts' accepting the position that benefit to the promisor can satisfy the requirement of consideration even where there is no obviously or practically discernible detriment to the promisee.

(c) *Williams v Roffey Bros*

All this emphasis on benefit to the promisor tends to outflank the reasoning of the old renegotiation cases, which had been that the promisee suffered no detriment (and so provided no consideration) by merely performing his earlier contract with the promisor. It sets the scene for, or culminates in, *Williams v Roffey Bros & Nicholls (Contractors) Ltd.*[32]

The case gives rise to two related problems: just what was going on, and how much has the outcome changed the law as previously understood.

(i) *Facts and Result*

The defendants were a firm of builders who had entered into a contract with a housing association to refurbish twenty-seven out of the twenty-eight flats in a block belonging to the association. For the purpose of performing that contract they had entered into a subcontract with Mr Williams under which he was to do the carpentry work on the flats for £20,000 payable in instalments. The subcontract did not specify the size of the instalments or specify when they were to be paid, but it was found at the trial that it was an implied term of the subcontract that interim payments should be related to the work done and be made at reasonable intervals. Mr Williams did a considerable amount of work on all the flats, nine were substantially completed, and £16,200 was paid to him. At this

---

[29] [1956] 1 WLR 496.   [30] [1957] 1 WLR 148.

[31] eg *Pitt v PHH Asset Management Ltd* [1994] 1 WLR 327, 332; *Simon Container Machinery v Embra Machinery AB* [1998] 2 Lloyd's Rep 428, 435; *Edmonds v Lawson* [2000] QB 501, 515.

[32] [1991] 1 QB 1.

stage he got into financial difficulties (partly, it seems, because of his own failure adequately to supervise his workmen and partly because the originally agreed price was unreasonably low) and the defendants promised to pay him an extra £10,300 at the rate of £575 for each of the remaining eighteen flats as work on each was completed (actually 18 × £575 = £10,350). They made this promise partly because they were afraid that Mr Williams would not be able to finish on time (and so expose them to penalties under their contract with the housing association) and partly because their own surveyor thought that the originally agreed price for Mr Williams's work was too low. In the surveyor's view a reasonable price for that work would have been £23,783 (about 19 per cent more than the originally agreed sum)—though that is scarcely a good reason for promising to pay him in all £30,300 (about 51.5 per cent more than the originally agreed sum). After being promised the extra £10,300, Mr Williams went on working but received only one further payment of £1,500; he then stopped work after having substantially completed work on eight more flats; and the courts evidently regarded his refusal to go on working as justified by the defendants' refusal to make any further payments. The defendants hired other carpenters to finish the work and incurred one week's penalty under their contract with the housing association. The trial judge held that Mr Williams was entitled to enforce the defendants' promise of an extra £575 for each of the eight flats completed after it was made (£4,600) less a deduction (unspecified) for defective work plus some further payment under the original contract. These sums came to the round figure of £5,000, from which was deducted the £1,500 already paid (since the new promise) making a recovery of £3,500 in all. The Court of Appeal affirmed this decision. The reason for the exact amount of the recovery cannot be deduced from the figures given in the report:[33] it was not discussed by the Court of Appeal.

---

[33] It is impossible to tell what the relation the sum awarded bore to the percentage 'uplift' under the promise of extra payment since the amount of work done on the flats which were *not* completed is not stated in the report.

(ii) *Relation to Earlier Cases*

The question with which the judgments in the Court of Appeal are mainly concerned is whether there was any consideration for the defendants' promise to pay the extra £10,300; and the answer given to that question was that Mr Williams had provided consideration by performing the obligation imposed on him by the original contract. The problem is, of course, how to reconcile this with *Stilk v Myrick*,[34] and all the members of the Court protest that they are not overruling or departing from that case. So, for example, Glidewell LJ says that the effect of the *Williams* case is to 'refine and limit' but not to 'contravene'[35] the earlier case, which Purchas LJ describes as a 'pillar stone of the law of contract'[36]—but proceeds to destabilize it by saying that the case 'might be differently decided today';[37] and Russell LJ, while being more openly critical of *Stilk v Myrick*, says that he does not base his judgment on any doubt 'as to the correctness of the law long ago enunciated'[38] in that case. This caution with regard to so old a case (of which there are conflicting reports) may seem somewhat strange, but of course we are not concerned simply with a decision at nisi prius in 1809; on the consideration point, the principle of *Stilk v Myrick* was many times followed, or recognized as good law, throughout the nineteenth and twentieth centuries.[39] How, then, does the Court of Appeal in the *Williams* case get round *Stilk v Myrick*? Five lines of reasoning can be extracted from the judgments:

1. The main reason for the decision in the *Williams* case, used by each member of the Court, was that there was consideration in the shape of the benefit obtained by the defendants in consequence of Mr Williams's continuing to do the work which he was already bound to do under the original contract. No doubt this line of reasoning is

---

[34] (1809) 2 Camp 317.   [35] [1991] 1 QB 1, 16.
[36] [1991] 1 QB 1, 20.   [37] Ibid 21.   [38] Ibid 19.
[39] For a recent example, see *Syros Shipping Co SA v Elaghill Trading Co (The Proodos C)* [1980] 2 Lloyd's Rep 390; cf the *Atlas Express* case [1989] QB 833 (*ante* at n 12).

supported by the traditional definition of consideration as detriment to the promisee *or* (in the alternative) benefit to the promisor. But how does it distinguish *Stilk v Myrick* and its progeny? In that case the promisor (the captain) also got a benefit: he got his ship home and no one suggested that this satisfied the requirement of consideration.

2. A second point (stressed particularly by Purchas LJ) was that there was no element of duress in the *Williams* case—ie no threat by Mr Williams to break his contract; on the contrary, it was the defendants' own surveyor who started the idea that the originally agreed rate of pay was too low. But there is nothing in either of the reports of *Stilk v Myrick* to suggest that the sailors there had made any threat to desert. The captain's promise was (so far as one can tell from the reports) just as spontaneous as that of the defendants in the *Williams* case—and a good deal less generous—only a little more than 20 per cent of the originally agreed wages of £5 per month, at least if we assume that all the members of the crew were paid at the same rate.

3. A third possibility is that *Stilk v Myrick* was based on public policy grounds which may in the early nineteenth century have affected crew agreements. But although there is support for this view in one of the reports of the case,[40] it is specifically denied in the other,[41]—and it is the latter report which is the only one referred to by the Court of Appeal in the *Williams* case.

4. A fourth possibility is (in the words of Russell LJ) to state 'the law long ago enunciated in *Stilk v Myrick*' in the form that 'a gratuitous promise pure and simple remains unenforceable unless given under seal'[42] (or, as we should now say, in a deed). But in *Stilk v Myrick* there is no reference to a 'gratuitous promise'; much less do we there find the phrase 'pure and simple'. Gratuitous promises lack consideration; but promises which lack consideration are not necessarily gratuitous. In *Stilk v Myrick* the promise was not gratuitous at all as the captain by means of it got a benefit for himself.

---

[40] 6 Esp 60.   [41] 2 Camp 317.   [42] [1991] 1 QB 1, 19.

5. A fifth possibility is that there was consideration of quite a different sort in the *Williams* case. The new agreement replaced 'a haphazard method of payment by a more formalised scheme involving the payment of a specified sum on completion of each flat'.[43] This reasoning does (in principle) satisfy the orthodox requirement of consideration as the new method *could* have benefited either party. But it is found in only one of the judgments, that of Russell LJ, and does not seem to be the main ground on which that judgment is based.

Nothing that I have said in this discussion of the difficulty of reconciling the two cases is intended as a criticism of the outcome in the *Williams* case. But I do suggest that it would have been better if the Court had rather more openly revealed or even emphasized that they were taking a different approach (from that of the earlier cases) to the consideration issue by relying on the element of benefit to the promisor and regarding it as sufficient even in the absence of detriment to the promisee. The point was well put by Hirst J (as he then was) in the *Anangel Atlas* case, where he said that as a result of the *Williams* case 'the law had undergone a radical development'.[44] His reasoning captures the essence of that case (if we allow for a pair of apparent misprints): 'Where there is a practical conferment of benefit ... for the promisee [promisor?] there is good consideration, and it is no answer to say that the promisor [promisee?] was already bound; where on the other hand there is a wholly gratuitous promise, *Stilk's* case remains good law'.[45] Clearly in this passage a promise which benefits the promisor is *not* regarded as 'wholly gratuitous'.

The outcome of all this is that (in the increasing pact cases) performance of a contractual duty owed by the promisee to the promisor can constitute consideration for the new promise if that performance in fact confers a benefit on the

---

[43] [1991] 1 QB 1, 19.

[44] *Anangel Atlas Compania Naviera SA v Ishikawajima—Harima Heavy Industries Co Ltd (No 2)* [1990] 2 Lloyd's Rep 526, 544.

[45] Ibid 545.

promisor. At the same time, it necessarily reduces the old protective function of the requirement of consideration; but in these cases this function is now more satisfactorily performed by the law relating to duress, including economic duress. All this seems to me to be a major new development and if there is a criticism to be made of the *Williams* case it is that it does little to bring the importance of that development home to the reader. In my view, the development is not only significant; it is, for two reasons, also beneficial. First, it makes the law internally more consistent in bringing the two-party cases into line with the three-party cases. Secondly, and this is the more important point, the development enables us to discard the public policy reasoning of some of the old cases and to replace it with the concept, now available, of economic duress. That, I suggest, is a more efficient tool or control mechanism since it applies only in cases of actual pressure, whereas public policy reasoning tended to invoke often unconvincing arguments of merely hypothetical pressure. There remains the further question whether this new mechanism is *adequate*, ie whether it deals with a sufficiently wide range of cases. I shall return to this question at the end of the discussion of variations which reduce obligations.

3. DECREASING PACTS

(a) Consideration and Duress

In this group of cases our starting points are first the old common law rule, going back to *Pinnel's* case[46] in 1602, that part payment of a debt cannot be any satisfaction of the whole; and secondly the rule that a promise to accept part payment in full settlement of a debt is not binding for want of consideration. One reason for the rule is that the debtor provides no consideration for that promise by merely paying less than the amount that he already owed. But

---

[46] (1602) Co Rep 177a.

again there is a public policy cross-current. If the promise were binding, the debtor might bring undue pressure to bear on the creditor, and we shall see that this policy consideration was relevant in one of the modern cases on this point, *D & C Builders v Rees*.[47]

(b) *Foakes v Beer*: Protection of Creditors

The case which settled the law as it stood at the beginning of the twentieth century was *Foakes v Beer* (in 1884);[48] and, though there was probably no element of undue pressure in this case, there were other factors which justified the outcome. In outline, the facts were that Mrs Julia Beer had in 1875 recovered a judgment against Dr John Foakes for £2,090 19s. which, by statute, bore interest at 4 per cent per annum. Sixteen months later Dr Foakes had paid little or nothing and was asking for yet more time to pay. The parties then, in 1876, entered into an agreement, drafted by Dr Foakes's solicitor,[49] which recited that Dr Foakes had 'requested the said Julia Beer to give him time to pay' and went on to provide that, 'in consideration of' Dr Foakes's paying £500 'in part satisfaction of the judgment debt' and 'on condition' of his paying instalments of £150 on 1 July and 1 January each year to Julia Beer or her nominee 'until the whole said sum of £2090.19s shall have been paid and satisfied . . . then the said Julia Beer undertakes and agrees that she will not take any proceedings on the said judgment'. By June 1882 Dr Foakes had paid £2,090 19s. and 'about that date' Mrs Beer claimed a further £360[50] (some £20,000 in today's money) by way of interest. At first instance Dr Foakes relied successfully on the 1876 agreement; but the Court of Appeal and the House of Lords held that this agreement was no bar to her claim. Two issues were discussed, first, what did the 1876 agreement mean? And secondly, what was its legal effect?

So far as the first issue was concerned, the question was

---

[47] [1966] 2 QB 617.   [48] (1884) 9 App Cas 605.
[49] Ibid 625.
[50] *Beer v Foakes* (1883) 11 QBD 221, 222.

whether the agreement meant that, if Dr Foakes paid instalments amounting to the principal sum, then Mrs Beer would not claim interest. There is nothing in the reports to indicate that Dr Foakes's liability to pay interest was discussed in the negotiations leading up to the 1876 agreement, and Lord Selborne doubted whether this issue was 'really present to the mind of'[51] Mrs Beer. Nevertheless he held that the operative part of the agreement was 'clear'— it said '£2090.19s' and not '£2019.19s plus interest'—and, that being so, the case was governed by the well-established rule that 'clear' words in the operative part of an agreement could not be controlled by recitals—ie here by the recital that Dr Foakes was asking for time. On the issue of construction, Lord Blackburn agreed with Lord Selborne; Lords Fitzgerald and Watson did not agree, but Lord Watson was prepared to assume that he was wrong on the construction point. There being no record of any speech from a fifth Law Lord, we have a majority of sorts in favour of Dr Foakes on the construction issue. But on the issue of the legal effect of the agreement the decision went in favour of Mrs Beer. She was not bound by her promise to forgo interest: Dr Foakes had provided no consideration for that promise by paying the principal sum since he was already bound to make that payment before the promise was made.

The actual decision in *Foakes v Beer* does not seem to be unjust. What seems to have happened was that Dr Foakes's solicitor dug a technical trap for Mrs Beer and the House of Lords arranged an equally technical rescue. The technical trap was the rule that recitals cannot control 'clear' words in the operative provisions of a contract. The technicality invoked to rescue her was the rule in *Pinnel's* case (as later interpreted) under which payment by Dr Foakes of part of what was due (the principal) could not constitute consideration for Mrs Beer's promise to forgo the rest (the interest). I call this a technical rescue because probably she did benefit in fact from the 1876 agreement. Lord Blackburn stressed this aspect of the case and was critical of the rule in *Pinnel's*

[51] (1884) 9 App Cas 605, 610.

case. But, being a good judge as well as a great lawyer, he did not dissent: he must have seen that the outcome proposed by the other members of the House was not unjust. Conversely, the reasoning of those others is, with respect, less than wholly convincing. They were not prepared to overturn the 'rule in *Pinnel's* case' because it 'has been accepted as part of the law of England for 280 years'.[52] Sometimes, that would be a strong argument. If a long-established rule is one on which people rely, there is a case for saying that it should not be overturned by judicial decision since such a reversal operates retrospectively and so defeats legitimate expectations, at least in the particular case. But is the 'rule in *Pinnel's* case' really of this kind? Do people rely on this rule, or if they do, should the law encourage them to do so? I doubt whether the antiquity of the rule was an adequate justification for continuing to apply it in the circumstances of *Foakes v Beer*. If there had been evidence of Mrs Beer's intention to exploit the rule as a weapon in the negotiations with Dr Foakes, I should have had little, if any sympathy with her. The fact that does engage my sympathy on her side is that, though she was probably not coerced, she does appear to have been tricked into making a promise which, on its true construction, had an effect not intended by her. The requirement of consideration was a useful tool for protecting her against trickery.

Equally, that requirement can be used to protect a creditor in such renegotiation cases against duress. This possibility is well illustrated by *D & C Builders Ltd v Rees*[53] where a small building company had, in the spring of 1964, done work on Mr Rees's shop and sent in its bill for the work in May and again in June. Payments on account were made, but some £480 remained due and reminders sent in October elicited no payment. On Friday 13 November Mrs Rees took a hand, phoned the builders, and said that her husband would pay £300 in full settlement. The builders, being 'in desperate financial straits' said they would take £300 now and give Mr Rees a year to find the balance, but

---

[52] (1884) 9 App Cas 605, 612.   [53] [1966] 2 QB 617.

Mrs Rees insisted that the receipt for £300 must be 'in completion of the account'. The report is not altogether clear on the question whether she also misrepresented her husband's and her financial position at this time.[54] The payment of £300 was made, a receipt in the required form was given, and then the builders sued for the balance of their charges. Two defences were raised: (i) bad workmanship, (ii) the agreement to accept £300 in full settlement of the £480. The second defence was tried as a preliminary issue and was rejected. Two members of the Court (Danckwerts and Winn LJJ) rejected it because, following *Foakes v Beer*, there was no consideration for the builders' promise to take part payment in full settlement. The third member of the Court (Lord Denning MR) did not, for reasons which will become obvious, want to base his decision on lack of consideration. Instead, he said that there was 'no true accord' because the settlement had been procured by 'intimidation',[55] ie by Mrs Rees's threat to pay nothing unless the builders would accept £300 in full settlement: 'She had no right to insist on his taking it in full settlement'.[56] Of course the difficulty is that no debtor has any such 'right to insist' and yet Lord Denning is (as will appear) anxious to uphold some such agreements. What was it that led him to the opposite view in the *D & C Builders* case? Was it that Mr Rees or his wife knew of the builders' 'desperate financial straits'? or that Mrs Rees, at least by implication, threatened to pay nothing if the builders would not give a receipt in full settlement? or that she misrepresented her husband's financial position (if she indeed did this, it is arguable that her conduct would now amount to a criminal offence)?[57] The answers to these questions are not clear from the report; but whatever they may be, the two approaches in the Court of Appeal are reminiscent of the two approaches to negotiation in the cases on

---

[54] Danckwerts LJ at p 626 suggests that there was such a misrepresentation but Winn LJ at p 627 says that there was no finding to this effect.

[55] [1966] 2 QB 617, 625.   [56] Ibid.

[57] That of by deception dishonestly securing the remission of any existing liability, contrary to Theft Act 1978, s 2(1)(a).

seamen's wages: that is of the 'consideration' and 'public policy' approaches.

Foakes v Beer and the *D & C Builders* case both show that consideration reasoning can perform a useful protective function. But such reasoning can apply even in the absence of any improper conduct on the part of the debtor (the promisee); and it may have been this fact which had led, even before *Foakes v Beer*, to criticism of the rule there to be applied as 'a most extraordinary peculiarity of English law',[58] and to the creation of a long list of exceptions to it at common law. It did not for example apply where the creditor's claim was disputed or unliquidated, or where the new agreement provided for some variation in the debtor's performance.[59] To adopt an expression used by Devlin J in another context,[60] only the most enthusiastic lawyer could take any satisfaction from the fact that the requirement of consideration is satisfied by the 'gift of a horse, hawk or robe',[61] whether together with or apart from any part payment, or by payment one day early, however large the agreed reduction of the debt may be. Even a nominal consideration such as the traditional peppercorn will do, so that this exception potentially destroys the protective force of the rule. The trouble with consideration reasoning is once again that it is too blunt an instrument: it may fail to protect the creditor where such protection ought to be given and, conversely, give him protection where none is or should be available. The first possibility can be illustrated by going back to the *D & C Builders* case and making the point that the defendant lost as a result of a simple error of tactics. The building work was done in the spring, the bill was first sent in May, and complaints about the work were made in November. The bill was for £746 13s. 1d. and it is unlikely that such an odd sum was agreed in advance. So the claim only became 'liquidated' by subsequent failure to query the amount. If the bill had been queried when

---

[58] *Couldery v Bartrum* (1881) 19 Ch D 394, 399.

[59] See Treitel, *The Law of Contract* (10th edn, 1999) 115–119.

[60] *Pyrene Co Ltd v Scindia Navigation Co Ltd* [1954] 2 QB 402, 416.

[61] *Pinnel's* case (1602) Co Rep 117a.

received, the demand would have been unliquidated; and if Mr or Mrs Rees had complained of defects at this time, instead of waiting until November, it would also have been disputed. So the rule in *Foakes v Beer* would not have applied. The builders might now (on such facts) be able to argue that they were victims of economic duress, but that concept was not accepted by English law until some ten years after the *D & C Builders* case came before the Court of Appeal.

(c) The *High Trees* Case

(i) *Facts and Decision*

The second possibility—that the creditor may be protected where no protection is or should be available—arises because the consideration reasoning makes no allowance for the fact that a renegotiation reducing the obligation of the debtor may be a perfectly reasonable transaction, concluded without any reprehensible conduct on the debtor's part.

That possibility brings us to the *High Trees* case,[62] where no element of either coercion or trickery affected the agreement which reduced the debtor's obligation. The *High Trees* case is surely one of the most prominent of the landmarks in twentieth century contract law; and the fact that it should have attained this status is, in many ways, remarkable. It was a decision at first instance in which, so far as I can tell, the judgment was unreserved: the reports indicate that the case was argued and decided on a single day, 18 July 1946; if there was any time for reflection, it could at most have been the luncheon recess. The report of the judgment in the Law Reports occupies just three pages. When he decided the case, Denning J had been a judge of the King's Bench Division for less than nine months and of the High Court for less than two and a half years.[63] The case became almost

---

[62] *Central London Property Trust Ltd v High Trees House Ltd* [1947] KB 130, [1947] LJR 77, (1946) 175 LT 333, (1946) 62 TLR 557, [1956] 1 All ER 256 n.

[63] Denning J was appointed to the High Court Bench on 9 March 1944 and transferred to the King's Bench Division on 24 October 1945.

immediately the subject of intense academic and judicial debate of which my own memories are particularly vivid as it was in full swing in Trinity Term 1947 when my first steps in the law of contract were being guided by the great Dr (then Mr) J. H. C. Morris, and when I had fairly recently learned that lower courts were supposed to follow decisions of the House of Lords. The importance of the case was instantly recognized in almost all parts of the legal establishment. I say 'almost' because of course there was an exception. The editors of the All England Law Reports (whose names I shall suppress) did not think the case worth reporting and it does not appear in that series for another ten years.[64] Meanwhile, it got quite enough exposure in the Law Reports, the Law Journal Reports, the Law Times Reports, and the Times Law Reports, which were first off the mark on 20 September 1946.[65]

It is not entirely clear exactly what lay behind the transactions in the *High Trees* case, but the facts so far as we can discover them from the reports were as follows. In 1937 a ninety-nine year lease of a new block of flats in London was granted at an annual rent of £2,500. The landlord and the tenant were associated companies, the landlord owning all the shares in the tenant. By the time the Second World War broke out in September 1939, the flats were not fully let and it became clear that this state of affairs was likely to continue for some time as many people had left London in anticipation of German air raids. So on 3 January 1940 the landlord agreed with the tenant to reduce the annual rent from £2,500 to £1,250, apparently with retrospective effect ('as from the commencement of the lease'). Curiously, this was the time of the 'phoney war'—the air raids on London did not begin in earnest until the summer of 1940, but the fear of them was keeping evacuees away. By the beginning of 1945 the flats were fully let even though the German bombardment of London by V2 rockets continued until nearly the end of the European war in May 1945. Meanwhile, the landlord company had not prospered: in 1941 its

---

[64] n 62 *supra*.   [65] Ibid.

debenture holders had appointed a receiver, whose successor in September 1945 gave notice to the tenant company claiming arrears of rent and the full rent for the future. The action was brought for £625 in respect of the two quarters ending 29 September and 25 December 1945. It was described as a 'friendly' action, no doubt because it was nominally between two companies one of which owned the other. But I wonder whether it was as friendly as all that. The substantial contest seems to have been between the tenant and the landlord's creditors, and the interests of these parties were very much opposed.

As in *Foakes v Beer*, two questions arose: one as to the meaning of the 1940 agreement and one as to its legal effect. On the first issue, Denning J held that the promise to reduce the rent was 'understood by all parties only to apply under the conditions prevailing at the time when it was made, namely when the flats were only partially let'.[66] In 1945 the lease still had over ninety years to run and the idea that the parties had in 1940 intended to cover the whole of that period was implausible. So the actual outcome was that the landlord's claim for the full rent in respect of the September and December 1945 quarters succeeded. But on the second issue Denning J held that the effect of the agreement for the periods during which it did apply was to prevent the landlord from claiming the full rent during that period. He relied on the principle derived from *Hughes v Metropolitan Railway*[67] under which a party to a contract may be precluded (at least temporarily) from enforcing his strict legal rights under it if he has made a promise to the other party not to do so, if he intended that promise to be binding and to be acted on by the promisee, and if the promisee did act on it. Before the *High Trees* case this 'reliance' principle had not been applied to promises unsupported by consideration[68] to accept part payment of a debt in full settlement;

---

[66] [1947] KB 130, 135.

[67] (1877) 2 App Cas 439, 448.

[68] The principle had been applied in *Buttery v Pickard* (1946) 62 TLR 241 to a promise to reduce rent but in that case the requirement of consideration can be said to have been satisfied by the tenant's forbearing to exercise a contractual right

the novelty of the case lay in its assertion that the principle applied to such promises, and that 'the logical consequence' was that 'a promise to accept a smaller sum in discharge of a larger sum, if acted upon, is binding notwithstanding the absence of consideration'.[69] But, setting aside the question whether the consequence is indeed logical, what about *Foakes v Beer*? In the Law Reports we find this single short sentence: 'That aspect was not considered in *Foakes v Beer*.'[70] Now the first point to be made about this sentence is that it is not to be found in any of the other four reports of the case so that the fascinating question arises whether it actually formed part of the apparently extempore judgment or was an afterthought, added when the editor of the Law Reports submitted his draft to the judge for approval. The second, and perhaps more significant, point is that it is hard to suppose that the House of Lords in *Foakes v Beer* can have been unaware of the principle in *Hughes v Metropolitan Railway* which had been decided only seven years previously, particularly as two members of the House of Lords who had decided the *Hughes* case[71] also heard the appeal in *Foakes v Beer*. The most plausible explanation of the fact that 'That aspect was not considered in *Foakes v Beer*' seems to be that it was not thought to be relevant since *Foakes v Beer* was concerned with the argument that legal rights had been *permanently* extinguished while the *Hughes* principle was concerned with their temporary suspension. All that is well-trodden ground which I do not wish to retraverse here.[72] I do, however, want to take up a number of points of continuing difficulty or controversy about the *High Trees* principle.

(ii) *Conflict with Protective Function*

First, there is the possibility that the reliance principle of the *High Trees* case can come into conflict with what I have called

---

to terminate the lease (though this was not the *ratio decidendi* of the case). The tenant had voluntarily resumed paying the full rent when the wartime conditions, which had been the ground for the reduction, came to an end.

[69] [1947] KB 130, 135.   [70] Ibid.

[71] Lords Selborne and Blackburn.

[72] See Treitel, *The Law of Contract* (10th edn, 1999) 120–122.

the protective function of *Foakes v Beer*. That is, the debtor may have made the part payment in reliance on the creditor's promise to accept it in full settlement; but that promise may have been obtained by means which can be described as disreputable. That was the position in the *D & C Builders* case[73] where it left Lord Denning in a dilemma. *Foakes v Beer* would have yielded the result that he wanted, but he did not want to reach it by that route. So he in effect says that *Foakes v Beer* has been trumped by the *High Trees* case but that the reasoning of the latter case applies only where it would be 'inequitable' for the creditor to go back on his promise; and that this requirement was not satisfied because the debtor (or his wife) had extracted the promise by 'putting undue pressure on the creditor'.[74] He uses the analogy of intimidation,[75] which is not quite exact,[76] but points in the right direction: as already suggested,[77] the question on facts such as those of the *D & C Builders* case would now be whether the promise had been obtained by economic duress. A wider notion of 'undue pressure' or abuse of superior bargaining position would probably be rejected as (in the words of Lord Scarman in an analogous context) 'unhelpful because it would render the law uncertain'.[78]

(iii) *The 'Estoppel' Analogy*

Secondly, the *High Trees* case and its numerous progeny are now often discussed under the heading of 'estoppel' or 'promissory estoppel', but it is, to say the least, very much open to doubt whether the principle was so classified by Denning J himself in the *High Trees* case. He mentions the familiar difficulty that *Jorden v Money*[79] had restricted the operation of estoppel to a representation of existing fact, so

---

[73] [1966] 2 QB 617.   [74] Ibid 625.

[75] *Rookes v Barnard* [1964] AC 1129.

[76] Intimidation is committed in situations involving *three* parties (eg where A induces B to act to the detriment of C by threatening to break A's contract with B). The *D & C Builders* case involved only *two* parties.   [77] p 26 *ante*.

[78] *Pao On v Lau Yiu Long* [1980] AC 614, 634.

[79] (1854) 5 HLC 185. This case is not cited in the briefly reported decision at first instance in *Re Wickham* (1918) 34 TLR 158, which is one of the authorities relied on in the *High Trees* case but is hard to reconcile with *Jorden v Money*.

excluding representations as to the future. From this it is clear that the type of estoppel that he had in mind was estoppel by representation. He then refers to some of the cases which he regards as applying the equitable principle that a party is (in some circumstances) precluded from acting inconsistently with a promise 'intended to be binding, intended to be acted on, and in fact acted on'.[80] He goes on to say that it is 'in that sense only, that such a promise gives rise to an estoppel'—that is, in the sense that the promisor is not allowed to act inconsistently with it—and that the cases on which he relies are 'not cases of estoppel in the strict sense'.[81] What lies behind these statements is a perception, perhaps not fully articulated, that this 'estoppel' is wholly different from estoppel by representation.

Let me try to explain. If a warehouseman represents that goods are in his warehouse when they are not, the estoppel to which the representation gives (or may give) rise prevents him from establishing the *fact* that the goods are not there. So, if in the *High Trees* case the tenant had represented that the flats were occupied when they were not, any estoppel which might have arisen would have precluded him from establishing that the flats were in fact empty. But the issue that arose in the *High Trees* case was not of this kind at all: there was no dispute about facts, even if we regard statements about the future (or promises) as 'facts', as the law relating to misrepresentation now quite commonly does. There was not even any dispute about whether a promise had been made or about the terms in which that promise was expressed. The only dispute was about the *legal effects* of a promise the existence and contents of which were not in dispute, that is about the question whether the promisor was in some sense bound by the promise even though it was not supported by consideration. The view that he was so bound is linked to estoppel by representation only in the very general sense that the law in many highly disparate cases regards it as unmeritorious for a person to take inconsistent positions.

---

[80] [1947] KB 130, 134.   [81] Ibid.

(iv) *Cause of Action?*

The distinction that I have just tried to draw is also relevant to the question whether the equitable principle invoked in the *High Trees* case is capable of giving rise to a cause of action. Where the estoppel is one by representation, there is a sense in which it cannot have this effect. That position is well illustrated by cases on the now repealed section 3 of the Bills of Lading Act 1855,[82] but to avoid the technicalities of that subject let me give an example based on a variation on my warehouseman case. Let us suppose that there are two warehousemen, A and B, and that A represents to a buyer or pledgee of goods that those goods are in B's warehouse, when they are not. Although A may be estopped from denying the truth of that statement, that does not make him liable to the buyer or pledgee as bailee of the goods and in this sense the estoppel does not give rise to a cause of action.[83] In my example warehouseman A might, in appropriate circumstances (eg if he were negligent), be liable for misrepresentation; but that liability is based on the fact that the statement was *false* while any liability by estoppel would be based on the opposite assumption, ie that the statement was *true*. That could be the position if the statement had been made by B: in that case our hypothetical buyer or pledgee would 'as a result of being able to rely on an estoppel, succeed on a cause of action [the bailment] on which, without being able to rely on that estoppel, he would necessarily have failed'.[84]

None of the above reasoning applies directly where the 'estoppel' relates (as in the *High Trees* case) not to any of the *facts* in issue but to the *legal effects* to be given to a representation or promise. Here we are not looking for a separate cause of action which would arise if the facts represented were true or if the promise had contractual force. We are simply asking whether there are legal grounds for, or

---

[82] See *Carver on Bills of Lading* (1st edn, 2001) §2-014.

[83] Cf *Low v Bouverie* [1891] 3 CL 82.

[84] *Amalgamated Investment & Property Co Ltd v Texas Commerce International Bank Ltd* [1982] QB 84, 131–132.

against, giving some remedy to the promisee, at least to some extent, by reason of his reliance on the promise. Let us suppose, in my case of two warehousemen, that one of them, A, says to the buyer or pledgee: 'Your goods are in B's warehouse; I shall go and collect them for you.' Let us further suppose that the promisee has relied on A's promise to collect the goods, that the statement that the goods are in B's warehouse is *true*, but that A's promise to collect them is not kept. Or let us suppose that the parties in the *High Trees* case had tried to solve the financial problems arising from the war in a different way—not by a rent reduction, but by the landlord's promising to take over the tenant's obligations under repairing covenants. If the landlord had failed or refused to perform that promise, it seems that Denning J would not have given the tenant any right of action merely by virtue of his reliance on the promise: 'the courts [he said] have not gone so far as to give a cause of action in damages for breach of such a promise';[85] and he was to repeat and apply that view in *Combe v Combe*.[86] They would merely have provided the tenant with a defence against the landlord's claim to forfeit the lease.

The difficulty of giving the promisee 'a cause of action in damages' on the promise in both my examples is, of course, that such a step runs the risk of coming into direct conflict with the rules of law which lay down the requirements for the creation, and the legal effects, of a binding contract. To some extent, that difficulty is reduced by restricting the equitable principle to cases in which 'the promise was intended to create legal relations' and Denning J explains *Jorden v Money* on the ground that 'there the promisor made it clear that she did not intend to be legally bound'.[87] No doubt, too, if the promise took the form of an offer calling for an acceptance (eg if in the *High Trees* case the landlord had written to the tenant proposing to halve the rent and had added 'Let us know whether this scheme is acceptable to you'), then the principle would not give rise to a cause of

---

[85] [1947] KB 130, 134.   [86] [1951] 2 KB 215 (p 37 *post*).
[87] [1947] KB 130, 134.

action if an acceptance were posted by the tenant and lost in the post.[88] From here we can take the next step and say that the same is true if the promise is not supported by consideration; and it was apparently the risk that the *High Trees* principle might come into conflict with this requirement that influenced Denning LJ in *Combe v Combe*.[89] There a promise made by a husband to his wife during divorce proceedings to pay her an annual allowance was first held not to have been supported by consideration and it was then also held that the wife could not invoke the *High Trees* principle as a ground for enforcing the promise: the principle, he says, 'never stands alone as giving a cause of action'.[90] That restriction on its scope had been foreshadowed in the *High Trees* case itself; and in *Combe v Combe* Denning LJ begins his discussion of the point by saying, 'Much as I am inclined to favour the principle of the *High Trees* case, it is important that it should not be stretched too far, lest it be endangered.'[91] The Mansfieldian echo[92] is clear and almost certainly deliberate. No doubt at this stage Denning LJ was anxious to avoid the rejection of the *High Trees* principle on the ground that it might come into head-on collision with the rule that a promise is not binding as a contract unless it is supported by consideration or made in a deed.

In most of the modern cases in which the doctrine has been invoked, the missing element (so to speak) of contract formation has been consideration; and perhaps for this reason the view has been expressed in some very recent cases that the rule that the 'estoppel' (ie the *Hughes* or *High Trees* principle) gives rise to no cause of action is restricted 'to the protection of consideration' and has 'no general application in the field of estoppel'.[93] But it is hard to see

---

[88] The principle of *Household, etc, Insurance Co Ltd v Grant* (1879) 4 Ex D 216 would apply.

[89] [1951] 2 KB 215.   [90] Ibid 220.   [91] Ibid 219.

[92] *Weston v Downes* (1778) 1 Dougl 23, 24 ('I am a great friend to the action for money had and received, and therefore I am not for stretching it lest I should endanger it').

[93] *Azov Shipping Co v Baltic Shipping Co* [1999] 2 Lloyd's Rep 159, 179; *Thornton Springer v NEM Insurance Co Ltd* [2000] 2 All ER 489, 519.

why this one requirement of contract formation should be singled out for special treatment; and the very latest, though no doubt not the last, word on the subject is that no cause of action is created by a 'promissory estoppel' where the promise is not of the degree of certainty required for the creation of a binding contract.[94]

Whatever view may be taken of the exact scope of what I shall call the rule in *Combe v Combe*, the point that I want to emphasize is that its rationale differs from that of the rule that, in cases of estoppel by representation, the mere fact that a person is precluded from denying the truth of something that he has said does not involve him in any liability. If A says that goods are in the possession of B, that statement does not turn A into a bailee of the goods and in that context the statement that estoppel does not create a cause of action makes perfectly good sense. If A makes a promise to B that is not supported by consideration, it does not in the same sense follow that A cannot to some extent be bound by the promise; the question whether and to what extent the promise is enforceable against A if B has acted in reliance on it is one of legal policy. One policy argument may be that enforcement of the promise can come into conflict with the rules as to contract formation, but obviously there are ways of meeting this point: eg by making the remedy on the promise discretionary or by merely *limiting* the promisor's power to go back on the promise as opposed to entirely taking that power away: ie by giving him the power to revoke it on giving reasonable notice.

(v) *Differences between Kinds of Estoppel*

The distinction between estoppels which relate to *facts* and those which relate to *legal effects* is also relevant to the continuing debate on the question whether the various types of estoppel which have, during the last century, played such a prominent part in the law of contract form part of a single general principle or whether a useful purpose is served in continuing to distinguish between

---

[94] *Baird Textile Holdings Ltd v Marks & Spencer plc* [2001] EWCA Civ 274 [38].

them. Lord Denning has taken the view that they can 'all
. . . now be seen to merge into one general principle shorn
of limitations'.[95] The opposing point of view has been
expressed in the statement of Millett LJ (as he then was)
that 'the attempt . . . to demonstrate that all estoppels . . .
are now subsumed in the single and all-embracing estoppel
by representation and that they are all governed by the
same principle' has 'never won general acceptance'.[96] If I
have to choose between these views, I shall declare myself
to be a respectful adherent of Lord Millett's view. The law
of contract in the twentieth century has been much
concerned with four types of estoppel. I shall call them
estoppel by representation, estoppel by convention,
promissory estoppel, and proprietary estoppel. The significant divide is between cases in which the estoppel prevents
a party from denying *facts* and those in which there is no
dispute about facts but only about the *legal effects* of a
proved or admitted promise. I have already put estoppel by
representation into the former category and I have no doubt
that estoppel by convention[97] also belongs there: it applies
to resolve the issue whether a promise has been made. Similarly, I have put promissory estoppel into the second category and I have no doubt that this is where proprietary
estoppel also belongs. The issue in proprietary estoppel
cases is as to the legal effect of a promise which is either
admitted or proved by evidence; it is not about *facts* which
the promisor is precluded from denying by means of an
estoppel. So there is a difference in legal nature between the
two groups; and when we come to the second group there
are, according to the authorities, many differences between
promissory and proprietary estoppel both in the conditions
in which they operate and in their legal effects.[98] Most
significantly, the principle that estoppel does not create a
cause of action does not apply to cases of so-called 'proprietary estoppel'. So if Mrs Jorden's proposed generosity in

---

[95] *Amalgamated Investment & Property* case (n 84 *supra*) [1982] 2 QB 73, 122.

[96] *First National Bank plc v Thomson* [1996] Ch 231, 236.

[97] See eg the *Amalgamated Investment & Property* case (n 95 *supra*).

[98] See Treitel, *The Law of Contract* (10th edn, 1999) 133–135.

favour of Mr Money had taken the form, not of saying that
she would not sue him on a bond, but of telling him that, on
his marriage, she would make him a gift of a cottage on her
estate and he had in reliance on that promise not merely
married but repaired the cottage roof, then he might, at
least subject to the court's discretion, have been able to
enforce her promise.[99] Even if we accept Denning J's explanation of *Jorden v Money* in the *High Trees* case[100] (that 'the
promisor made it clear that she did not intend to be legally
bound') that would not preclude the operation of proprietary estoppel: this doctrine has been successfully invoked
in a number of cases precisely because the arrangement
between the parties had been made in a 'family' context
and therefore had no contractual force for want of contractual intention.[101] Exactly why proprietary estoppel can give
rise to a cause of action while promissory estoppel cannot is
not made at all clear in the English cases. One possible
explanation is that the proprietary estoppel cases originally
involved an element of unjust enrichment (though some
modern cases apply the doctrine even in the absence of this
factor), while promissory estoppel could arise from mere
action in reliance by the promisee; and that this was
regarded as a less strong ground (than unjust enrichment)
for relief.

What the examples I have given, and the authorities,
seem to show is that the various kinds of estoppel are
governed by different rules both as to their requirements
and as to their legal consequences. No doubt the view that
they 'merge into one general principle'[102] may encourage
cross-fertilization between them, but it can equally encourage cross-infection and even cross-sterilization; and it is not
beyond the bounds of argument that *Combe v Combe* may
illustrate the latter process. And the phrase 'shorn of limitations'[103] does set alarm bells ringing at least for those who
set any store by the value of predictability in the law. This

---

[99] Treitel (n 98 *supra*), 130–133.   [100] [1947] KB 130, 134.
[101] eg *Dillwyn v Llewelyn* (1862) 4 DF & G 517; cf *Crabb v Arun DC* [1976] Ch 179,
where the promise was not sufficiently certain to give rise to a contract.
[102] *Ante* at n 95.   [103] Ibid.

seems to me to remain a desideratum, even if not in quite the same sense as that in which 'certainty' is in some contexts said to be an important requirement in commercial law. In those contexts, the purpose of 'certainty' is to enable parties to act in reliance on rules of law (for example, where a contractual term is classified as a 'condition').[104] That is not quite the point here: there would be little merit in going back on a promise in reliance on a rule to the effect that the promise was not legally enforceable, except perhaps where the promise was in terms expressed not to be legally binding (though even in cases of this kind there is controversy about agreements for the sale of land 'subject to contract').[105] The problem in the present context of 'one general principle shorn of limitations' is that such a principle, or at least its last three words, make it impossible to tell, even *after* all the relevant events, what the legal consequences of action on reliance on the promise will be. You have to go to court to find out. The distinction between the various types of estoppel of course does not entirely solve the problem of predictability, but it does reduce it to more manageable proportions and promotes an orderly solution by making it possible to develop a system of rules governing each of the different kinds of situation to which the four kinds of estoppel apply. They are linked only by the broadest of general principles, that the taking of inconsistent positions is, in some situations, to be discouraged by the law. A very recent statement from Lord Goff sums up the point to perfection: 'I am inclined to think that the many circumstances capable of giving rise to an estoppel cannot be accommodated within a single principle and that it is unconscionability which provides the link between them.'[106]

---

[104] See p 119 *post*.
[105] *Cohen & Nessdale* [1981] 3 All ER 112, 128, affirmed [1982] 2 All ER 97 ('a social and moral blot on our law'); Law Commission Paper No 65.
[106] *Johnson v Gore Wood & Co* [2001] 1 All ER 481, 508.

4. CROSS-OVERS

This discussion of the variation of contracts by subsequent agreement between the parties began with the distinction between increasing and reducing pacts. In the nineteenth century, legal effect was denied to each for want of consideration: this requirement was thought not to have been satisfied because, in each type of case, the promisee did no more than perform what was already owed to the promisor. In law, this was thought to be no detriment to the promisee nor (it seems) any benefit to the promisor, though other factors then called public policy and now more generally called economic duress were never far below the surface. So the sailors lost in *Stilk v Myrick*[107] and the creditor won in *Foakes v Beer*.[108] In the twentieth century there were two significant changes of approach. An increasing pact was enforced in *Williams v Roffey Bros*[109] on the ground that the requirement of consideration was satisfied because the promisor had in fact benefited, as a result of the promise, by securing actual performance of the promisee's original obligations. In the *High Trees* case,[110] some effect was given to a decreasing pact, even though there was no consideration, on the ground that the promise was intended by the promisor to induce, and had induced, reliance by the promisee and that therefore it was wrong to allow the promisor to go back on it: this reliance principle has become known as promissory estoppel. These developments give rise to a final question or pair of questions: can we apply the reasoning of the one line of cases in the other? That is, can we use *High Trees* reasoning in the increasing pact cases, illustrated by *Stilk v Myrick*, or *Williams v Roffey Bros* reasoning in the decreasing pact cases, illustrated by *Foakes v Beer*?

(a) *High Trees* and Increasing Pacts

The answer to the first of these questions has already been

---

[107] (1809) 2 Camp 317.   [108] (1884) 9 App Cas 605.
[109] [1991] 1 QB 1.   [110] [1947] KB 130.

discussed. The sailors in *Stilk v Myrick* were trying to use the captain's promise to found a cause of action, and so long as *Combe v Combe*[111] survives they cannot do this in English law. There is support for this view in *The Proodos C*[112] where consignees of goods promised to make certain extra payments to the carrier and it was held that a claim for those payments was not enforceable under the doctrine of promissory (or 'equitable') estoppel. The only slight difficulty, on the authorities, is that one of the judgments[113] in *Williams v Roffey Bros* does refer to the *Amalgamated Investment & Property* case, the leading modern case on a different type of estoppel, that is, on estoppel by convention. But the decision in the *Williams* case is not based on estoppel; it is based on the view that the requirement of consideration was satisfied; and the issue in relation to which estoppel was discussed in the *Amalgamated Investment & Property* case simply had no counterpart in the *Williams* case. That issue was whether a promise in a guarantee of money due to one bank also covered a loan made by one of the bank's subsidiaries: in other words it related to the question whether a promise of the latter kind *had been made*. In the *Williams* case, there was no issue of this kind: there was no doubt that the promise of extra payment had been made, nor was there any doubt as to its true construction. So I respectfully question whether the *Amalgamated Investment & Property* case was relevant to any of the issues in the *Williams* case, though counsel cannot be blamed for raising the point.

(b) *Williams v Roffey Bros* and Decreasing Pacts

The answer to the second question—can the reasoning of the *Williams* case be used in the context of a reducing pact such as that in *Foakes v Beer*?—is not so (relatively) easy. It is, moreover, still worth asking, even if *Foakes v Beer* has been to some extent bypassed by the *High Trees* case, since

---

[111] [1951] 2 KB 215.   [112] (n 39 *supra*) [1980] 2 Lloyd's Rep 390.
[113] [1991] 1 QB 1, 17 (Russell LJ).

the effect of a contractually binding variation is in a number of ways more favourable to the promisee than that of 'promissory estoppel'.[114] The essence of the reasoning in the *Williams* case was that performance by the promisee of an antecedent contractual duty which he owed to the promisor may in fact benefit the promisor and therefore suffice to satisfy the requirement of consideration. That may be true also of *partial* performance of the promisee's original duty and it was this very point which drove Lord Blackburn to the verge of dissent in *Foakes v Beer*: 'All men of business, whether merchants or tradesmen, do every day recognise and act on the ground that prompt payment of part of their demand may be more beneficial to them than it would be to insist on their rights and enforce payment of the whole. Even where the debtor is perfectly solvent and sure to pay at last, this is often so. Where the credit of the debtor is doubtful, it must be more so.'[115] Can we now say that part performance of the promisee's original obligation may, if it in fact benefits the promisor, constitute consideration for a reducing pact, and in particular for one to accept a smaller sum in satisfaction of the larger sum originally due? The answer given on the authorities falls into two parts: (1) yes it can, (2) so long as the benefit consists of something other than receipt of the part payment itself.

The first part of the proposition is supported by the *Anangel Atlas* case,[116] where a shipbuilder's promise to reduce the price payable by the buyers was held to have been supported by consideration moving from the buyers; and one way in which the buyers had provided consideration was by accepting the ship on the day fixed for delivery, even though they were already bound by the contract to do so. This benefited the builders in that the buyers in question were 'core customers' and their refusal to accept delivery might have adversely affected the builder's relations with other customers or potential customers. Note that this

[114] See Treitel, *The Law of Contract* (10th edn, 1999) 109–110.
[115] (1884) 9 App Cas 605, 622.
[116] (n 44 *supra*) [1990] 2 Lloyd's Rep 526.

reasoning differs from the old argument that the addition of a hawk, a horse, or a robe[117] might make the reducing promise binding. Those are things which the debtor was *not* already bound to do; accepting the ship was something that the buyers *were* already bound to do but the builder benefited because of its tendency: *pour encourager les autres.*

The second part of my proposition is supported by *Re Selectmove*,[118] where the original obligation had not been created by contract and the actual question was whether the creditor, the Inland Revenue, was bound by a promise to accept, not *part*, but *late*, payment, two instalments of which had actually been made. The Court of Appeal held that the reasoning of the *Williams* case did not apply since *Foakes v Beer* stood in the way: to say that the benefit of part payment constituted consideration 'would in effect leave the principle of *Foakes v Beer* without any application'.[119] Nor could that principle be avoided by saying (as Denning J had, or may have, said in the *High Trees* case) that 'That aspect was not considered in *Foakes v Beer*':[120] the factor of benefit to the promisor 'was a matter expressly considered in *Foakes v Beer* and yet held not to constitute good consideration in law'.[121]

The distinction between the two parts of my proposition—between cases in which the benefit to the creditor consists of part payment and those in which it consists of performance of some other antecedent obligation—may not seem to be very edifying; but the only way of avoiding it would be the reconsideration of the rule in *Foakes v Beer* and its possible reversal by the House of Lords. Would anything be lost if such a reversal took place? The rule no doubt has a protective function in cases such as *D & C Builders Ltd v Rees*, though in that kind of situation the same function could perhaps now in many cases be performed by the concept of economic duress. But that concept may not go far enough. There was, I repeat, nothing wrong with the

[117] *Ante* at n 61.   [118] [1995] 1 WLR 474.   [119] Ibid 481.
[120] [1947] KB 130, 135 (p 32 *ante*).
[121] [1995] 1 WLR 474, 481.

outcome in *Foakes v Beer*;[122] and I do not see how the case could be brought within even the expanding concept of duress; nor is it obvious what other legal machinery could be used to achieve the same end. Rectification has been suggested as a possibility[123] but this would work only if *both* parties had no intention that interest should be given up or if Dr Foakes *knew* that Mrs Beer had no such intention or if he was guilty of fraud or other unconscionable conduct in procuring the agreement.[124] But there was no evidence of any such circumstances so that the problem cannot be solved in this way. There is much to be said against *Foakes v Beer* but also something in its favour. How the balance will one day, perhaps in the twenty-first century, be struck continues to be a matter of speculation.

[122] p 25 *ante.*
[123] Smith & Thomas, *A Casebook on Contract* (10th edn, 1996) 245.
[124] See *Faraday v Tamworth Union* (1917) 86 LJ Ch 436; *Garrard v Frankel* (1862) 30 Beav 445, 451; *Commission for the New Towns v Cooper (Great Britain)* [1995] Ch 259.

2

The Battle over Privity

The most significant doctrinal development in English contract law in the twentieth century was no doubt the outcome of what I shall call the battle over privity. This discussion of it will be largely based on two leading House of Lords cases: the *Midland Silicones*[1] case and *Beswick v Beswick*.[2] By way of introduction, let me try to state where the law stood at the beginning of the period. By that time *Tweddle v Atkinson*[3] was widely regarded as having established the general rule that rights arising under a contract could be enforced only by the parties to it; a third party could not enforce such rights even though the parties intended that he should be entitled to do so. Whether *Tweddle v Atkinson* actually was authority for that proposition was indeed open to doubt;[4] and there were earlier authorities that supported a contrary view.[5] But in 1885 Bowen LJ declared that it was 'mere pedantry'[6] to cast doubt on the general common law rule; and that may be taken to be the generally accepted view at the beginning of the twentieth century. Two years before *Tweddle v Atkinson* a contrary development had been initiated in the United States by the New York case of *Lawrence v Fox*,[7] but this seems to have attracted little (if any) attention in England. It is curious to note that, although English cases denying the third party's right[8] were cited in *Lawrence v Fox*, admittedly only by the

---

[1] [1962] AC 446.   [2] [1968] AC 58.

[3] (1861) 1 B & S 393.

[4] For a judicial expression of such doubts, see *Darlington BC v Wiltshier Northern Ltd* [1995] 1 WLR 68, 77, *per* Steyn LJ.

[5] See eg *Dutton v Poole* (1678) 2 Lev 210, affirmed T Raym 302.

[6] *Gandy v Gandy* (1885) 30 Ch D 56, 69.   [7] 20 NY 268 (1859).

[8] eg *Price v Easton* (1833) B & Ad 433.

dissentients, the compliment was not returned in *Tweddle v Atkinson*, which contains no reference to *Lawrence v Fox*; nor was any reference made to any other foreign system. I shall have more to say later about transatlantic influences. The rejection of a third party beneficiary doctrine might be thought to have left a significant gap in English law, especially when compared with other systems; but there were many exceptions to the general rule and a skilled lawyer was unlikely to have serious difficulties in working his way round it.

So far I have referred only to the general rule of English law that a third party could not take the *benefit* of a contract. The doctrine of privity was also invoked to support the converse proposition that a third party was not *bound* by a contract. In one sense, this point is so obvious that it scarcely needs stating. A contract by which A promises B that C will pay £10 to B clearly cannot impose any obligation on C. But it is not nearly so obvious that a promise by A to B may not restrict C's freedom of action in some other way: eg by limiting his right to deal with the subject matter of the promise. This aspect of this problem goes back to *De Mattos v Gibson*; [9] exactly where the law stood on this point at the beginning of the century is not at all clear and even a hundred years later this uncertainty persists. [10] Another aspect of the problem will be more fully discussed below: [11] this concerns the enforceability of exemption clauses against persons who are not parties to the contract in which they are contained.

In the early part of the century both aspects of the doctrine of privity were applied in a series of cases concerning minimum price maintenance agreements, that is agreements designed to ensure that goods should not be sold by retailers for less than a minimum price specified by the manufacturers. Since manufacturers commonly sold to

---

[9] (1858) 4 De G & J 276.

[10] See *Lord Strathcona SS Co v Dominion Coal Co* [1926] AC 108; *Port Line Ltd v Ben Line Steamers Ltd* [1958] QB 146; *Law Debenture Trust Corp v Ural Caspian Oil Corp* [1993] 1 WLR 138, reversed on another ground [1995] Ch 152.

[11] pp 70–82 *et seq post*.

wholesalers who resold to retailers, privity here gave rise to difficulties: a minimum price term in the contract between manufacturer and wholesaler did not bind the retailer since he was not a party to it; while the manufacturer could not enforce such a term in the contract between wholesaler and retailer since he in turn was not a party to that contract. The subsequent legislative history of price maintenance agreements would take me too far from my theme, especially now that that topic is submerged in the very deep waters of the Competition Act 1998. There is, indeed, an argument that there was an undercurrent of public policy in these cases. The argument appears in one of the attacks later launched by Denning LJ on the doctrine of privity, in which he argues that a third party should be entitled to enforce a promise made for his benefit 'provided that he has a sufficient interest to enforce it', and he adds that such an interest 'does not include the maintenance of prices to the public disadvantage'.[12] But there is no trace of such reasoning in the leading case on the topic; and price maintenance agreements were not, even between the immediate parties to them, invalid as contrary to public policy at common law, though it took a few more years to establish this point.[13]

The best known of the price maintenance cases is *Dunlop v Selfridge*[14] where the manufacturer sued to enforce the contract between wholesaler and retailer; and the House of Lords rejected the claim without even calling on counsel for the retailer. The opposing views there expressed about the outcome of the case can be seen to reflect the positions taken in future debates. On the one side, there was Lord Haldane's well-known statement that 'In the law of England, certain principles are fundamental. One is that only a person who is a party to a contract can sue upon it. Our law knows nothing of a *jus quaesitum tertio* arising by

---

[12] *Smith and Snipes Hall Farm v River Douglas Catchment Board* [1949] 2 KB 500, 519.

[13] *Palmolive Co (of England) v Freedman* [1928] Ch 264. Cf Lord Dunedin's use of the words 'not in itself unfair' in the passage cited at n 16, *infra*.

[14] *Dunlop Pneumatic Tyre Co Ltd v Selfridge & Co Ltd* [1915] AC 847.

way of contract.'[15] On the other side there is Lord Dunedin's criticism—not, in fact, of the doctrine of privity, but of the doctrine of consideration (which played a more prominent part than the doctrine of privity in the reasoning of the House of Lords)—as making it 'possible for a person to snap his fingers at a bargain deliberately made ... not in itself unfair and which the person seeking to enforce it has a legitimate interest to enforce'.[16] Neither of these statements is entirely persuasive. On the one hand, Lord Haldane gives no reasons for the 'fundamental' principle; on the other hand, Lord Dunedin seems to exaggerate. Neither the doctrine of consideration, nor for that matter the doctrine of privity, made it possible for the retailer to 'snap his fingers at a bargain deliberately made'. The bargain was made with the wholesaler, who could have enforced it. He might, indeed, have had difficulty in obtaining damages since the law with regard to damages in respect of a third party's loss was then in a comparatively undeveloped state; and it is doubtful whether even now such a claim would on similar facts be available,[17] even apart from the complexities of competition law. But the retailer's promise to the wholesaler was a negative one and so in principle enforceable by injunction without proof of financial prejudice to the wholesaler.[18] To use the current metaphor, Lord Dunedin was not faced with a legal black hole.[19] The actual claim was for liquidated damages of £10 and an injunction.

2. THE TRUST EXCEPTION

Lord Haldane, after the passage quoted above, continued: 'Such a right [ie a *jus quaesitum tertio*] may be conferred by

---

[15] *Dunlop v Selfridge* (n 14 *supra*) 853. For a similar statement by Lord Macnaghten, see *Keighley Maxsted & Co v Durant* [1901] AC 240, 245.

[16] [1915] AC 847, 855.

[17] The situation in *Dunlop v Selfridge, supra,* is far removed from that in *Linden Gardens Trust v Lenesta Sludge Disposals Ltd* [1994] 1 AC 85 and from that in the *Darlington* case (n 4 *supra*).

[18] *Kemp v Sober* (1851) 1 Sim (NS) 517; *Marco Productions Ltd v Pagola* [1945] KB 111.

[19] See the *Darlington* case [1995] 1 WLR 68, 79; for the origins of this metaphor, see *Alfred McAlpine Construction Ltd v Panatown Ltd* [2001] 1 AC 518, 529.

way of property, as, for example, by way of trust'[20]—a reference to the equitable rule, going back into the eighteenth century,[21] that where a promisee had taken the promise as trustee for the third party, then the third party could enforce the promise against the promisor, joining the promisee as a party to the action (unless the promisor waived this requirement). This device had been applied in a number of nineteenth century cases,[22] and was again recognized and applied in 1925 by the House of Lords in *Walford's* case,[23] where it enabled a shipbroker to enforce a term in a charterparty for the payment of commission to him even though he was not a party to that contract; though another explanation of the case (for which there is a good deal of support in the speeches) is that the broker *was* a party to the contract, at least so far as it related to payment of commission, through the agency of the charterer.

The next year (1926) Arthur Goodhart, soon to become Professor of Jurisprudence at Oxford, became editor of the *Law Quarterly Review* and four years later still (in 1930) an article appeared in that journal by the great American contract lawyer Corbin.[24] The article was mainly about the English cases on trusts of promises; and I do not know what prompted Corbin to write it or to have it published in England, but the explanation may well lie in the association between Goodhart and Corbin at the Yale Law School, where Goodhart was a visiting professor in 1928–9. The gist of Corbin's arguments was that the 'trust of promise' reasoning amounted to the recognition of a third party beneficiary doctrine in equity, that on this point there was accordingly a conflict between common law and equity, and that the equitable principle prevailed by virtue of the

---

[20] [1915] AC 847, 853.
[21] *Tomlinson v Gill* (1756) Amb 330.
[22] eg *Lloyd's v Harper* (1880) 16 Ch D 290.
[23] *Les Affréteurs Réunis SA v Leopold Walford (London) Ltd* [1919] AC 801; Lord Atkinson heard this appeal as well as that in *Dunlop v Selfridge* (n 14 *supra*).
[24] (1930) 46 LQR 12.

general statement then contained in section 25(11)[25] of the Judicature Act 1873 giving primacy to the rules of equity in cases of such conflict. But this reasoning did not convince the English courts. In 1943 Corbin's article was cited to Uthwatt J in *Re Schebsman* by no less distinguished an advocate than Denning KC; but Corbin's reasoning was specifically rejected by the court.[26] Uthwatt J's decision was approved on appeal[27] without any further explicit reference to Corbin's article by the Court of Appeal even though it was again cited to that Court. The English courts came to view the cases based on 'trust of promises' reasoning as an exception, of limited scope, to the privity doctrine, rather than as a conflicting rule. A footnote to this little piece of history may be of some interest. Corbin's article was republished, in substance, as chapter 46 of his great treatise on *Contracts* in a volume bearing the publication date 1951. There he is quite unperturbed by *Re Schebsman*, referring to Uthwatt J (in a quaint anachronism) as a judge 'at *nisi prius*'[28] and saying nothing about the approval of his decision on appeal. So American scholars of the highest distinction[29] continue to cite Corbin's article as though it represented, even now, an accurate account of what I shall (I hope with greater accuracy) call the trust of promises *exception* to the common law privity doctrine.[30] Denning KC was elevated to the High Court Bench[31] soon after the Court of Appeal's decision in *Re Schebsman*;[32] and in his later judicial attacks on the doctrine of privity he sometimes invoked the *American* third party beneficiary doctrine[33] but

---

[25] Now Supreme Court Act 1981, s 49(1).   [26] [1943] Ch 366, 368.

[27] [1944] Ch 83, 104.   [28] *Corbin on Contracts* (1951), 854 n 64.

[29] Langbein, 105 Yale LJ 625, 646–647 (1997).

[30] Lord Atkinson (see n 23 *supra*) saw no conflict between common law and equity on the point so as to attract the operation of Judicature Act 1873 s 25(11).

[31] On 9 March 1944.   [32] Given on 6 December 1943.

[33] See his statement in *Drive Yourself Hire Co (London) Ltd v Strutt* [1954] 1 QB 250, 274 that American courts had 'followed the original *common law*, which is much more in accord with the needs of a civilised society' (italics supplied). The reference is to those cases before *Tweddle v Atkinson* (*supra* at n 3) which had upheld the third parties' claims.

he no longer relied on Corbin to support his own view of the *English* law on the point.

3. EARLY ATTACKS ON THE DOCTRINE

Those attacks were launched in two Court of Appeal decisions of 1949[34] and 1954[35] in which Denning LJ (as he had by then become[36]) disputed the existence of the doctrine of privity, and in this he had the support of Devlin J (as he then was)—curiously enough in a case[37] in which the issue was not whether a third party was entitled to the *benefit* of a term in a contract to which he was not a party, but whether the third party was *bound* by such a term. The term in question was a limitation of liability clause; and so we are led to the questions to what extent exemption and limitation clauses can either benefit or adversely affect third parties.

4. THIRD PARTIES CLAIMING THE BENEFITS OF EXEMPTION CLAUSES

(a) Vicarious Immunity and Bailment on Terms

The starting point for discussing the first of these questions is the still controversial *Elder Dempster* case.[38] A contract for the carriage of goods by sea was made between the time charterers of a ship and a cargo-owner on terms which exempted not only the charterers but also the shipowner from liability for bad stowage; and the outcome was that the shipowner was entitled to the benefit of the exemption clause even though he was not a party to the contract of carriage. So far as I know, there has been no serious challenge to this outcome on the merits; debate about the *Elder Dempster* case has concentrated on the more abstract problem of

---

[34] *Smith and Snipes Hall Farm v River Douglas Catchment Board* [1949] 2 KB 500.

[35] *Drive Yourself Hire Co. (London) Ltd v Strutt* [1954] 1 QB 250.

[36] On 14 October 1948.

[37] *Pyrene Co Ltd v Scindia Navigation Co Ltd* [1954] 2 QB 402.

[38] *Elder Dempster & Co v Paterson Zochonis & Co* [1924] AC 522

reconciling the decision with the doctrine of privity. In the Court of Appeal, Scrutton LJ[39] had approached this problem by creating a new exception to that doctrine, an exception which came later to be called the principle of vicarious immunity. This was that a servant or agent of a contracting party is entitled to the same exemptions and limitations, in performing the contract, as are available under it to his employer or principal. This reasoning received considerable support in the House of Lords;[40] but the decision there can also be explained on the ground that there was a contract between the cargo-owner and the shipowner made through the agency of the charterers for one of these parties,[41] or (and this is the explanation now preferred[42]) that, in the words of Lord Sumner, there was a bailment between cargo-owner and shipowner 'on terms which include the exceptions and limitations of liability stipulated in the known and contemplated form of bill of lading'.[43] The bailment arose when the cargo-owner presented the cargo for loading to the shipowner who, the charter being a time charter, at this stage took charge of it and then performed the carriage *operation* even though he was not a party to *contract* of carriage between charterer and cargo-owner. That 'bailment' reasoning leaves two questions: first, the legal nature of the bailment relationship; and, secondly, the mechanism by which the bill of lading terms came to be incorporated into that relationship.

With regard to the first question, one view with distinguished judicial support from Devlin and Diplock JJ and Morris LJ was that, on receipt of the goods and signature of the bill of lading by the captain (the shipowner's

---

[39] [1923] 1 KB 420, 441–442, dissenting on another point (viz whether the damage to the goods had been caused by bad stowage) on which his view was upheld by the House of Lords.

[40] [1924] AC 522, 534 (*per* Lord Cave, with whom Lord Carson agreed) 548 (*per* Lord Finlay, dissenting on other grounds).

[41] [1924] AC 522, 534.

[42] *Scruttons Ltd v Midland Silicones Ltd* [1962] AC 446, 470; *KH Enterprise v Pioneer Container (The Pioneer Container)* [1994] 2 AC 324, 335; *The Mahkutai* [1996] AC 650, 667–668.

[43] [1924] AC 522, 564.

employee), an *implied contract* came into being between shipowner and cargo-owner;[44] and so these parties were brought into a direct contractual relationship with each other. A second view, with equally distinguished judicial support, mainly from Lord Goff, is that the bailment is non-contractual[45] and so capable of producing legal consequences even in the absence of privity of contract. Neither view of the nature of the bailment relationship entirely solves the problem of the incorporation of the bill of lading terms into that relationship, particularly as the bill of lading in the *Elder Dempster* case was expressed to have been signed by the captain[46] as agent, not of the shipowner, but of the charterers. Probably the incorporation took place on the analogy of the incorporation of terms into contracts by custom or usage. This seems to be the force of Lord Sumner's reference to 'the known and contemplated form of bill of lading'.[47]

However all that may be, it is clear that the 'bailment on terms' reasoning of the *Elder Dempster* case was narrower in scope than the 'vicarious immunity' reasoning. The latter required no bailment, nor any *legal explanation* of how the terms of the contract between the employer and the customer came to be incorporated into any relationship between the customer and the employee. The 'vicarious immunity' reasoning simply *asserts* that the employee is protected by a contract to which he is not a party. It gives a policy reason for this conclusion but does not attempt to explain the legal mechanism by which it is reached. The policy reason is stated by Scrutton LJ in the *Elder Dempster* case: 'Were it otherwise there would be an easy way round the bill of lading in the case of a chartered ship; the owner of the goods would simply sue the owner of the ship and ignore the bill of lading exceptions.'[48] This may be convincing where each of the three parties has bargained with at

---

[44] *Pyrene Co Ltd v Scindia Navigation Co Ltd* [1954] 2 QB 402, 406; *Scruttons Ltd v Midland Silicones Ltd* [1959] 2 QB 171, 187; *Adler v Dickson* [1955] 1 QB 158, 199.

[45] *The Pioneer Container* [1994] AC 324, 335; *The Mahkutai* [1996] AC 650, 662.

[46] See *Scruttons Ltd v Midland Silicones Ltd* [1962] AC 446, 455.

[47] [1924] AC 522, 564.   [48] [1923] 1 KB 420, 441–442.

least one of the others on a basis of equality and on terms which contain no surprises. But it was much less convincing in personal injury cases, particularly where the injured party had contracted as a consumer.

Our next group of twentieth century cases is of this kind. These cases arose out of contracts for the carriage of passengers made before exemption clauses were subject to the legislative controls which now restrict their validity and may indeed penalize their use.[49] The best known of these cases is *Adler v Dickson*[50] where Mrs Adler was a passenger on the cruise liner *Himalaya* and was injured, while attempting to reboard the ship, as a result of the alleged negligence of members of the crew. She was a widow and any judicial sympathy that she may have engaged on that account was evidently not outweighed by her having been also a first class passenger. The terms of her ticket exempted the carriers from liability 'in respect of any injury . . . to the person of the passenger . . . while the passenger is embarking or disembarking' and it was held that this provision was no bar to her action in tort against the carriers' employees. The principle of vicarious immunity would have led to a different result, but the Court of Appeal declined to apply that principle, partly because it did not regard the principle as forming the *ratio decidendi* of the *Elder Dempster* case, and partly because there were policy reasons *against* it. In evident response to an argument similar to that of Scrutton LJ in the *Elder Dempster* case (quoted above)[51] Jenkins LJ said[52] that it would be 'far more absurd' to impute to the passenger who had contracted on terms exempting the *shipowner* from liability an intention to deprive herself of all right to redress against the shipowner's *servants* for their

[49] See especially Unfair Contract Terms Act 1977; Unfair Terms in Consumer Contracts Regulations 1999; Consumer Transactions (Restriction on Statements) Order 1976 (as amended).

[50] [1955] 1 QB 158.

[51] At n 48 *supra*; cf Lord Finlay in the *Elder Dempster* case [1924] AC 522, 548: 'It would be absurd that the owner of the goods could get rid of the protective clauses of the bill of lading in respect of stowage, by suing the owner of the ship in tort.'

[52] [1955] 1 QB 158, 187.

negligence 'however gross'. Similar policy reasons against the principle have been expressed in Australia and the United States;[53] and it may be no accident that what seems to be the first judicial use of the phrase 'vicarious immunity' occurs in an opinion of Holmes J in which he said that there was '*no* such doctrine as vicarious immunity from liability for torts'.[54] The conflict of policies continues to be unresolved. In Canada the Supreme Court in the *London Drugs*[55] case applied a form of the vicarious immunity principle in favour of employees of a warehouseman and held that they were protected by a limitation of liability clause in a contract between their employer and the owner of goods stored in the warehouse. The decision was based in part on the reasoning that, if the employees were not protected, then the owner of the goods would be able to 'circumvent or escape the limitation of liability to which it had expressly consented'.[56] This is much the same point as that on which Scrutton LJ had relied in the *Elder Dempster* case.[57] Perhaps one reason why this policy prevailed over that on which Jenkins LJ had relied in *Adler v Dickson* was that in the *London Drugs* case the goods-owner was not only aware of the limitation clause but could also have avoided it by making a declaration of value and paying an extra charge.[58] The question whether English courts will follow the *London Drugs* case remains an open one;[59] my present point is that they could do so without rejecting the policy reasoning of Jenkins LJ in *Adler v Dickson*, where Mrs Adler had no such option under her contract as London

---

[53] *Wilson v Darling Island Stevedoring Co* [1956] 1 Lloyd's Rep. 346, 359; *Robert C Herd v Krawill Machinery Corp* 359 US 297, 303 (1959).

[54] *AM Collins & Co v Panama R Co* 197 F 2d 893, 897 (1952) (italics supplied); the statement is made in a dissenting opinion but the majority decision was overruled in the *Robert C Herd* case (n 53 *supra*).

[55] *London Drugs Ltd v Kuehne & Nagel International Ltd* [1992] 3 SCR 299.

[56] Ibid 441.

[57] *Supra* at n 48.

[58] In the *Midland Silicones* case [1962] AC 446 the shippers (whose rights the claimants had acquired on transfer of the bill of lading) would have had a similar choice under s 4(5) of the US Carriage of Goods by Sea Act 1936, giving effect to the Hague Rules, but no reliance is placed on this point in the speeches.

[59] See *The Mahkutai* [1996] AC 650, 665.

Drugs had under theirs. The point retains its practical importance even after the passing of the Contracts (Rights of Third Parties) Act 1999 since it is, to say the least, doubtful whether the contract in either of these two cases was so drafted as now to confer rights of 'enforcement' on the third parties, the employees.[60] It should be added that, in a number of contexts, the question is now in part resolved by legislation extending the protection of exemptions and limitations in a contract to the servants or agents of a contracting party. This is true, for example, where the contract is one for the carriage of goods by sea contained in or evidenced by a bill of lading governed by the Hague-Visby Rules.[61] But this provision does not apply in favour of an independent contractor and so would not cover a situation such as that in the *Elder Dempster* case.

(b) Rejection of Vicarious Immunity: The *Midland Silicones* Case

Nor, for the same reason, would the Hague-Visby Rules provisions in favour of third parties apply to facts such as those in the *Midland Silicones* case,[62] which differs from the cases so far discussed in that it raises issues with regard to both of the aspects of the privity problem: that is, not only with regard to the 'benefit', but also with regard to the 'burden', aspect. A drum of silicones had been shipped on a vessel belonging to United States Lines under a contract contained in or evidenced by a bill of lading in which the claimants were named as consignees. The bill incorporated the United States Carriage of Goods by Sea Act which gave effect to the Hague Rules and so limited the liability of 'the carrier' to $500 per package. On transfer of the bill of lading, property in the goods passed to the claimants and at the same time rights and duties under the bill of lading were transferred to them. The drum was then damaged by the negligence of a firm of stevedores who had been

---

[60] ie whether the requirements of ss 1(1)(a), 1(2), and 1(3) were satisfied.
[61] Carriage of Goods by Sea Act 1971, Sch, art IV bis (2).
[62] *Scruttons Ltd v Midland Silicones Ltd* [1962] AC 446.

engaged by United States Lines to unload the ship and to deliver the goods to the consignees; I shall deal later with the exact circumstances in which the damage occurred. The contract between United States Lines and the stevedores also contained an exemption clause: it provided that the stevedores were 'to have such protection as is afforded by the terms, conditions and exceptions' of the bill of lading. The stevedores admitted liability but relied on the $500 limitation of liability. So two questions arose: were the stevedores entitled to the *benefit* of the limitation clause in the contract between the carriers and the consignees? And were the consignees *bound* by the limitation clause in the contract between the carriers and the stevedores? The House of Lords answered both questions in the negative as the stevedores were not parties to the first, nor the consignees parties to the second, contract.

On the first point, the stevedores were defeated by the doctrine of privity of contract, as stated by Lord Haldane in *Dunlop v Selfridge*, which was relied on not only by Lord Simonds, but also by Lords Reid and Morris[63] and so was taken to have survived the judicial attacks made on it in the 1940s and 1950s.[64] None of the reasons which had protected the third party in the *Elder Dempster* case availed the stevedores in the *Midland Silicones* case: the carriers had not acted as agents for the stevedores in contracting with the cargo-owners since the contract of carriage made no mention of the stevedores; there was no 'bailment on terms' since the stevedores were never bailees of the goods; and the principle of vicarious immunity was not a recognized exception to the privity doctrine in English law. The agency point calls for no further comment, but something more should be said about the bailment and vicarious immunity points.

Rejection of the bailment argument turns on what may perhaps be called the special facts of the case. The relevant facts were that the drum had been unloaded from the ship and placed in a shed rented by the carriers from the Port of

---

[63] Ibid 467, 473, 494.   [64] *Supra* at nn 34–37.

London Authority; the consignees had asked the carriers and then the Port Authority for delivery of the drum, and the damage was done while the stevedores were moving or attempting to move the drum from the shed into the lorry sent by the consignees to collect it. There was in these circumstances no bailment of the drum to the stevedores as they had never been entrusted with possession of it. If the shed had been rented by the stevedores, there would have been a bailment to them and they would have been sub-bailees of the consignees, at least if one can overlook the not inconsiderable difficulty that the bailors were not the consignees but the shippers of the drum.[65] But would such a bailment relationship have given the stevedores the benefit of the limitation of liability? There is, indeed, some support in a dictum in the *The Pioneer Container* for the view that a sub-bailee may be entitled to the benefit of an exemption clause in the head bailment—but only if the head bailor has *consented* to the inclusion of the clause into the sub-bailment. In the *Midland Silicones* case, the argument that there was an implied *contract* to this effect was rejected because (in the words of Lord Reid) 'if they [the consignees] had read the bill of lading, they would find nothing to show that the shippers had agreed to limit the liability of the stevedores'.[66] The same reasoning would negative the consignees' *consent* to the incorporation of any such term into even a non-contractual bailment.

My first comment on the rejection of the vicarious immunity argument in the *Midland Silicones* case is that this part of the reasoning of the majority is, so to speak, entirely abstract: it is presented simply as a deduction from Lord Haldane's statement of the privity doctrine in *Dunlop v Selfridge* and from the earlier decision in *Tweddle v Atkinson*. None of the policy reasons for or against vicarious immunity is discussed, at least explicitly. It is true that Lord Simonds says[67] that he agrees with 'every line and every

---

[65] See *Carver on Bills of Lading* (1st edn, 2001) §§7–104 to 7–106.
[66] [1962] AC 446, 474.
[67] Ibid 472.

word' of the judgment of Fullagar J in a similar Australian case[68] and in that judgment a policy ground for rejecting vicarious immunity, similar to that given by Jenkins LJ in *Adler v Dickson* quoted above,[69] can be found: a 'self-confessed tortfeasor' should not be allowed to 'shelter behind a document that is no concern of his'. And perhaps there is a policy argument implicit in Lord Reid's description of the *Elder Dempster* case (at least in so far as it is based on vicarious immunity) as an 'anomalous and unexplained' exception to 'the general principle that a stranger cannot rely for his protection on provisions in a contract to which he is not a party'.[70] Why is this exception anomalous when other exceptions to the privity doctrine are recognized earlier in the same speech as 'well-established'?[71] Is it because it lacks a satisfactory legal rationale or because it is in itself undesirable? The latter explanation is scarcely satisfactory because Lord Reid's speech contains suggestions for ways round the privity doctrine, suggestions which were to bear fruit in the later drafting of Himalaya clauses and in judicial recognition of their legal effectiveness.[72]

There is another difficulty in treating the doctrine of privity as the decisive ground for rejecting the principle of vicarious immunity. In the United States the principle of vicarious immunity has also been rejected even though there is no doctrine of privity. In *Robert C Herd v Krawill Machinery*,[73] the Supreme Court, on facts similar to those of the *Midland Silicones* case, reached the same result and based it on policy considerations: in particular, on need to maintain the principle of an agent's personal liability 'unless exonerated . . . by a statute or a valid contract binding the person damaged';[74] and on the need to construe exemption and limitation clauses strictly against the person

---

[68] *Wilson v Darling Island Stevedoring and Lighterage Co* [1956] 1 Lloyd's Rep 346, 559.

[69] *Supra* at n 52.   [70] [1962] AC 446, 479.

[71] Ibid 473.   [72] pp 64–70 *et seq post*.

[73] 359 US 297 (1959).

[74] Ibid 303; immunities created *by contract* (as opposed to those created *by law*) were evidently not regarded as falling within Restatement, Agency §347; see *Carver on Bills of Lading* (1st edn, 2001) §7–021.

seeking to rely on them.[75] The stevedore lost because he was 'not a party to *nor a beneficiary of* the contract of carriage'.[76] It was not open to the House of Lords to investigate the second of these possibilities;[77] but in the United States the stevedore could have succeeded on the ground that he was a beneficiary, even if he was not a party. Perhaps the reason why the majority in the *Midland Silicones* case did not discuss the underlying policy is that there is no substantial policy issue in any of these cases. As Scrutton LJ had said in the *Elder Dempster* case, 'the real question is which set of underwriters should bear the loss'.[78] I should not be surprised to learn that even Mrs Rose Adler had travel insurance (though that would probably not cover her pain and suffering).

Lord Denning, as is well known, dissented in the *Midland Silicones* case. He refers,[79] in the first place, to Scrutton LJ's statement in the *Elder Dempster* case of what came to be called the principle of vicarious immunity[80] and he seeks to provide a doctrinal basis for it on the ground of voluntary assumption of risk. On that basis, he admits that the principle would not help the stevedores in the *Midland Silicones* case because the bill of lading was expressed so as to protect only the carrier. But (he continues), 'if the bill of lading were expressed in terms by which the owner of the goods consented to take on himself the risk of loss in excess of $500, whether due to the negligence of the carrier or the stevedores, I know of no good reason why his consent, if freely given, should not be binding on him'.[81] In all this reasoning, Lord Denning seems to be guarding his flank. He disliked some exemption clauses fully as much as he disliked the doctrine of privity and so he does not want to take a position inconsistent with *Adler v Dickson*,[82] where he had been a member of the court. He achieves consistency by

---

[75] 359 US 297, 305.   [76] Ibid 308 (italics supplied).

[77] See pp 66, 104 *post* for the position under the Contracts (Rights of Third Parties) Act 1999.

[78] *Elder Dempster* case [1923] KB 420, 442.   [79] [1962] AC 446, 482–483.

[80] *Supra* at n 39.   [81] [1962] AC 446, 489.

[82] [1955] 1 QB 158.

saying that 'it is not so easy to find an assent by a passenger to take the risk of personal injury on himself'[83] and by concluding that in both cases there was no such consent because the contracts in them did not in terms exempt, or limit the liability of, the third parties. Five years later, in the Court of Appeal in *Beswick v Beswick*,[84] he seems slightly to have shifted his ground. There he says that generally a third party can enforce a contract made for his benefit (joining the promisee to the action) but that 'it is different if he has no legitimate interest as when he is seeking to rely on an exemption clause to exempt himself from his just liability. He cannot rely on an exemption clause in a contract to which he is not a party.'[85] The *Midland Silicones* case is loyally accepted, without criticism, for this last proposition; there is no longer any qualification for the case in which the promisor's consent to the term exempting the third party is 'freely given'.[86]

The outcome of Lord Denning's reasoning on the present point in the *Midland Silicones* case is that the stevedores *could* have been protected by the bill of lading terms without being in any contractual relationship with the cargo-owners, though on the facts they *were* not so protected as the cargo-owners had not consented to their being so protected. One might think that this was not all that far away from Lord Reid's reasoning, which also suggests that a differently worded bill might (if certain other requirements were satisfied) have protected the stevedore,[87] a suggestion that was to lead to the development of Himalaya clauses.[88] But there is a fundamental difference in the legal reasoning behind the two approaches. Under Lord Reid's reasoning, the stevedore is protected because (and only if) he is brought into a contractual relationship with the cargo-owner. Under Lord Denning's reasoning, he would be protected as a third party beneficiary, even though there was *no* contract between himself and the cargo-owner.

---

[83] [1962] AC 446, 489. [84] [1966] Ch 538. [85] Ibid 557.
[86] *Supra* at n 81. [87] [1962] AC 446, 474 (pp 67–68 *post*).
[88] pp 64–70 *post*.

Lord Denning's speech goes on with a most uncharacteristic remark: 'I suppose, however, that I must be wrong about all this: because your Lordships, I believe, take a different view.'[89] His dissent is based, not on the view that the stevedore is entitled to the *benefit* of a term in the contract between cargo-owner and carrier; but on the view that the cargo-owner is *bound* by terms of the contract between carrier and stevedore. The reasoning is that the carrier is bailee of the goods; and that as such he can bind the owner by terms of a contract which the carrier has made with a subcontractor 'in regard to' the goods if those terms are 'such as [the owner] expressly or impliedly authorised, that is to say, consented to be made'.[90] It is not at all easy to see why the cargo-owner who (according to a previous part of the speech) had *not* consented to take the risk of loss in excess of $500 resulting from the stevedore's negligence by virtue of his *own* contract with the carrier should be taken to have consented to a term to this effect in the contract between carrier and stevedore, of which he was unaware. The other members of the House of Lords discuss the same issue of the cargo-owner's consent in the context of the argument that there was an implied contract between cargo-owner and stevedore. Their conclusion (already mentioned[91] and to be more fully discussed below[92]) was that there was no evidence of such consent either in the terms of the bill of lading or in other circumstances; and this seems, with respect, to be convincing. Even so, this part of Lord Denning's dissent contains the germ of an idea that was to have long-term consequences, as we shall see.

(c) Ways round Privity: Himalaya Clauses

The outcome of the *Midland Silicones* case was far from popular. There were, I think, two causes of dissatisfaction. First, the application of the privity doctrine might cause liability to rest on an individual employee occupying a relatively

---

[89] [1962] AC 446, 489.   [90] Ibid 491.
[91] p 60 *ante.*   [92] p 71 *post.*

humble position in the organization protected by the exemption or limitation clause. This was no doubt a factor influencing the decision in the *London Drugs*[93] case; and in *Adler v Dickson*[94] the Court of Appeal was saved from discomfort on this score only by the employers' undertaking to 'stand behind' their employees if the Court should decide that the employees were not protected by the exemption clause.[95] Secondly, the outcome was liable to cut across insurance arrangements which were probably based on the assumption that insurance for loss above the financial limits specified in the contract and caused in the course of the performance of the carriage operation would be covered by the cargo-owner's insurance, whether the loss was caused by the personal fault of the carrier or by his employees or by a subcontractor. As already noted, in contracts for the carriage of goods by sea legislation has now provided a partial solution of this problem by extending 'defences and limits of liability which the carrier is entitled to invoke under [the Hague-Visby] rules' to his servants or agents;[96] but this solution does not extend to independent contractors (such as the stevedores in the *Midland Silicones* case or the shipowners in the *Elder Dempster* case). That development did not take place until some ten years after the decision in the *Midland Silicones* case; meanwhile a solution that was more comprehensive was developed by contractual draftsmanship.

In the United States there was no doctrinal difficulty about drafting a way round the rule in the *Robert C Herd* case. This rule denied the third party the protection of the limitation clause on the ground that he was 'not a party to nor a beneficiary of the contract'.[97] It followed that, if the contract made him a '*beneficiary*' of the term limiting or excluding liability, then he could rely on it even though he

---

[93] (n 55 *supra*) [1992] 3 SCR 299.　　　　　[94] [1955] 1 QB 158.

[95] Cf *Norwich CC v Harvey* [1989] 1 WLR 828, 834, where it was said that if the contract negatived the third party's duty then 'neither can any of their employees have' owed a duty. No further consideration is given to this point in the judgment: see *post*, p 70.

[96] Art IV bis (2) (n 61 *supra*).　　　　　[97] 369 US 297, 308 (1959).

was not a *party* to it. Six years later, in the *Carle Montanari* case, an American court accordingly drew the conclusion that 'the parties to a bill of lading may extend a contractual benefit to a third party by clearly expressing their intent to do so'.[98] The clause in that case was in fact somewhat more elaborate than this statement required it to be, containing declarations of agency and trusteeship, but any other way of expressing the requisite intention would in principle have sufficed. This would also now be true in England under the Contracts (Rights of Third Parties) Act 1999, though the relevant provisions of that Act would not solve by any means all the third party problems that can arise in cases of this kind.[99]

But under the English common law, the simple solution of naming the third party (such as an employee) as a person who was to have the benefit of the term did not work: the doctrine of privity stood in the way. A more elaborate device, known as a Himalaya clause (after the ship which Mrs Adler was about to reboard when she sustained her unfortunate accident) was devised, in response to suggestions made by Lord Reid in the *Midland Silicones* as to how persons who were not parties to the bill of lading contract might be protected.[100] The legal effect of such a clause is not to treat the third party as a beneficiary of a contract between two others; it is, on the contrary, to provide a framework for creating a *separate* collateral contract directly between one of the parties to main contract of carriage and the person who, though not a party to that contract, sought to rely on one of its terms.[101] That party, where the device operates, is no longer a third party: he is an immediate party to a collateral contract with one of the parties to the main contract (usually with the shipper or those claiming under him) in which the Himalaya clause is contained.

---

[98] *Carle Montanari Inc v American Export Isbrandtsen Lines Inc* 275 F Supp 76, 78 (1967).

[99] See ss 1(1) and (6), 6(5) 'tailpiece'. The last two provisions apply only terms which *exclude or limit* liability.   [100] [1962] AC 446, 474.

[101] *New Zealand Shipping Co Ltd v AM Satterthwaite & Co Ltd (The Eurymedon)* [1975] AC 154.

Himalaya clauses are not entirely uniform in their wording; but their essential feature (so far as bill of lading contracts are concerned) is that they declare the carrier to have acted as agent for his servants, agents, and subcontractors for the purpose of securing to such persons the benefit of the carrier's exemptions from and limitations of liability. In *The Eurymedon*[102] the contract contained such a clause and the goods were damaged by the stevedore's negligence while being unloaded from the ship. It was held that a contract had come into being between cargo-owner and stevedore (giving the latter the benefit of the bill of lading exemptions and limitations) apparently through the mechanism of an offer made by the cargo-owner to the carrier acting as agent for the third party (the stevedore) and accepted by the latter when it performed the requested service by discharging the goods. There is some dispute on the question whether the contract is 'initially unilateral',[103] as Lord Wilberforce said, or bilateral, as Barwick CJ said in another case of this kind in a dictum[104] later approved by Lord Goff.[105] My preference is for Lord Wilberforce's view since it avoids the consequence of the stevedore's being in breach of a separate contract with the cargo-owner if he has justifiably terminated his contract with the carrier on account of the latter's breach and consequently refused to unload the goods.

The Eurymedon has been repeatedly followed; but difficulty has arisen (usually to be surmounted) in connection with a passage from Lord Reid's speech in the *Midland Silicones* case in which he sets out four requirements to be satisfied in cases of this kind for creating a contractual relationship between the wrongdoer and the injured party.[106] The first two requirements are that the bill of lading must make it clear that the third party is intended to

---

[102] n 101 *supra*.   [103] [1975] AC 154, 167–168.
[104] *Salmond & Spraggon (Australia) Pty Ltd v Joint Cargo Service Ltd (The New York Star)* [1979] 1 Lloyd's Rep 298, 304–305; Barwick CJ dissented from a judgment of the High Court of Australia that was reversed on appeal to the Privy Council: [1981] 1 WLR 138.
[105] *The Mahkutai* [1996] AC 650, 664.   [106] [1962] AC 446, 474.

be protected by the bill of lading contract, and that the bill must make it clear that the carrier is 'contracting as agent for the [third party] stevedore that these provisions should apply to the stevedore'. These requirements raise no more than points of drafting; neither was satisfied in the *Midland Silicones* case while both are satisfied by the typical Himalaya clause. Lord Reid's fourth requirement was that there must be 'consideration moving from the stevedore'. This requirement no longer presents any difficulty. One of the points decided in *The Eurymedon*[107] was that performance by the promisee (the stevedore) of an act could constitute consideration for a promise even though the promisee was already bound by a contract with someone other than the promisor to do that act; and this view has not since that case been judicially questioned. So the stevedore's act of unloading the goods and delivering them to the cargo-owner was consideration for the cargo-owner's promise to grant the stevedore the exemptions and limitations of the bill, even though the stevedore was already bound by its contract with the carrier to do these acts. The source of the difficulty is the third of the requirements in Lord Reid's list: that the carrier must have 'authority from the stevedore to do that, or perhaps later ratification would suffice'. In other words, there must not only be a declaration of agency by the carrier, but also prior authority from the third party (or 'perhaps' ratification). One can see the doctrinal reason for this latter requirement and also the practical need for it where the new collateral contract would impose *obligations* on the third party: this clearly cannot be done without that party's authority or consent. But where (as I have argued) the new contract is unilateral and its only effect is meant to be to give the third party the *benefit* of an exemption or limitation clause, it is hard to see what practical purpose is served by the requirement of prior authorization, or why Lord Reid is so hesitant about ratification.

---

[107] n 101 *supra*.

(d) Ways round Privity: Other Drafting Devices

Himalaya clauses are by no means the only drafting devices by which the third party can be protected. Another suggestion comes from Lord Roskill's speech in the *Junior Books* case,[108] which, as is well known, concerned the relationship of building owner, main contractor, and subcontractor. Although no issue of limitation or exclusion of liability arose in that case, Lord Roskill said that a 'relevant exclusion clause in the main contract . . . according to the manner in which it was worded might in some circumstances limit the duty of care'[109]—ie the duty owed in tort by the subcontractor to the building owner. That suggestion has been subjected to a good deal of criticism: one view is that Lord Roskill really intended to refer to an exclusion clause in the *sub*contract;[110] another is that where the hypothetical clause was contained 'in a contract to which the plaintiff [was] a party but the defendant [was] not', the defendant could not rely on it as there was no privity between these parties.[111] I am not convinced by these objections. So far as the first goes, it seems to me to be *less* plausible to say that the owner is bound by a term in the subcontract, over which he has little if any control, than to say that he is bound by a term in the main contract (to which, *ex hypothesi*, he has consented). So far as the second goes, it has more force where a person is alleged to be *bound* by a term of a contract to which he is not a party than where it is alleged that a person my *benefit* from a term in such a contract. Lord Roskill's suggestion makes (with respect) perfectly good sense where the subcontractor knows of the term in the main contract and that term in effect defines what he is required to do: for example, to store goods in a yard when, apart from the term in the main contract, it would have been more prudent to store them in a shed. In a number of

---

[108] *Junior Books Ltd v Veitchi Co Ltd* [1983] AC 520.
[109] Ibid 546.
[110] *Muirhead v Industrial Tank Specialities Ltd* [1986] QB 507, 525.
[111] *Leigh & Sillavan Ltd v Aliakmon Shipping Co Ltd (The Aliakmon)* [1986] AC 785, 815.

cases Lord Roskill's dictum has accordingly been applied. For example in *Norwich CC v Harvey*[112] building owners by a term in the main contract accepted the risks of fire and it was held that roofing subcontractors were not liable for fire damage either: 'though there was no privity of contract between the employers and the subcontractors ... the subcontractors contracted [with the main contractors] on a like basis'.[113] The subcontractors therefore *owed no duty* in respect of fire damage; and, the court went on, 'then neither can any of their employees have done so'.[114] This last point is taken as obvious: no one seems to have spared a thought for *Adler v Dickson*.[115]

Lord Roskill's dictum would not, I think, have helped the stevedores in the *Midland Silicones*[116] case. The dictum refers to a *'relevant* exclusion clause'—that is to one that 'might ... limit ... the duty of care'. A limitation clause is not of this kind. It does not specify what a person is required to do; it deals only with the legal consequences of his failing to do it.

5. BINDING THIRD PARTIES BY EXEMPTION CLAUSES

(a) The General Rule

The *Midland Silicones*[117] case is chiefly remembered as a decision on the point that the stevedores were precluded by the doctrine of privity from taking the benefit of an exemption clause in the contract between carrier and cargo-owner. But there is the further significant aspect of the case that there was also an exemption clause in the contract between stevedores and carriers; and the majority held that the stevedores could not rely on this clause against the cargo-owners because the cargo-owners were not parties to that contract and so not bound by its terms. The majority seem to take this point so much for granted that they deal with it

---

[112] [1989] 1 WLR 828.   [113] Ibid 834.   [114] Ibid.
[115] [1955] 1 QB 158 (p 56 *ante*).   [116] [1962] AC 446.
[117] *Supra* n 116.

only very briefly and in the context of the question whether there was an implied contract between stevedores and cargo-owners. Lord Simonds in this context says that 'They [the cargo-owners] knew nothing of the relations between the carrier and the stevedores,'[118] which is the nearest he comes to alluding to the contract between these two parties. Lord Reid is somewhat more explicit: 'There was in their [the stevedores'] contract with the carrier a provision that they should be protected, but that could not by itself bind the consignee . . . A provision in the contract between them and the carrier is irrelevant in a question between them and the consignee.'[119] The point is accepted as axiomatic. Lord Morris is equally concise in dealing with the point. He says it can have 'no effect with regard to the issues raised in this appeal'.[120] It is perhaps of some interest to note that he makes no reference to the cargo-owners' not being *parties* to the contract between stevedores and carriers; the point on which he relies is that the cargo-owners 'had *no knowledge* of the existence or of the terms of the stevedoring contract'. Lord Keith makes no reference to the point at all. Perhaps the majority's brevity in dealing with this aspect of the case is due to the fact that the point does not, so far as one can tell from the reports, have featured in the argument of counsel for the stevedores. That argument was entirely directed towards showing that the stevedores could take the *benefit* of a term in *the contract between the cargo-owners and the carriers*; it was rejected by the majority and also, apparently, in the end by Lord Denning. In so far as the majority deal at all with the point that the cargo-owners might be *bound by a term in the contract between carriers and stevedores*, they seem to be responding, not to counsel, but to what Lord Denning had to say on this point. No doubt they had seen his dissenting speech in draft before preparing the final versions of their own.

The principle that a person is not bound by exemptions and limitations in a contract to which he is not a party

---

[118] [1962] AC 446, 467.   [119] Ibid 474, 493.   [120] Ibid 493.

appears again in *The Aliakmon*[121] where goods were shipped by a seller under a bill of lading evidencing a contract of carriage between seller and carrier. The goods were then damaged through the carrier's negligence after the risk, but before the property, in them had passed to the buyer, so that the loss fell on him. He had no claim in contract because the conditions then required for transfer of contractual rights under bills of lading had not been satisfied;[122] and his tort claim against the carrier was rejected on the ground that, when the goods were damaged, he had no proprietary or possessory interest in them. One policy argument for rejecting the tort claim was that, if it succeeded, the carrier would be deprived of the protection of the Hague Rules, which formed part of the bill of lading contract. It was to rebut this argument that the buyer argued that he *was* bound by the exemptions and limitations of the contract of carriage. We seem here to be on the wrong side of the looking glass: normally, it is the person claiming the protection of the exemption clause (the carrier) who argues that the third party is bound; here this argument is put forward by the third party, to improve his chance of success in his tort claim. The House of Lords rejected the argument on the ground that the buyer was not (and had not become) a party to the contract of carriage; and so one reason for dismissing the buyer's tort claim was that its success would have deprived the carrier of the protection of the Hague Rules. The reasoning is not entirely free from difficulty since it does not take a great deal of ingenuity to think of a case in which the third party *has* acquired a proprietary or possessory interest in the goods without having become a party to the contract of carriage.[123] In that event, the main reason given

---

[121] [1986] AC 785 (n 111 *supra*,).

[122] He could not invoke s 1 of the Bills of Lading Act 1855 as property in the goods had not at the relevant time passed to him. On the facts of the case the buyer would now acquire contractual rights against the carrier on the bill of lading terms by virtue of Carriage of Goods by Sea Act 1992 s 2(1): *White v Jones* [1995] 2 AC 207, 265.

[123] eg if property had passed, but the bill of lading had not been transferred to him.

in *The Aliakmon* for dismissing the tort claim would not apply and the carrier, if liable to such a claim,[124] would be deprived of the protection of the Hague Rules.

(b) Ways round the General Rule

It is this possibility that Lord Denning in his dissenting speech in the *Midland Silicones* case called 'a serious gap in our commercial law'.[125] The particular gap with which he was there concerned was that it would be possible to 'turn the flank'[126] of the Hague Rules if some way were not found of binding at least some third parties by the exceptions and limitations contained in the Rules; but the problem is by no means confined to cases involving these Rules or other similar carriage conventions. It can arise out of any situation in which commercial relations affecting three persons are governed by two contracts to each of which only two of these persons are parties. In practical terms, this is the problem that worried Scrutton LJ in the *Elder Dempster* case when he referred to 'an easy way round the bill of lading'[127] though in legal terms his solution differed from that proposed by Lord Denning: Scrutton LJ wanted to give the wrongdoer *benefit* of a contract to which he was not, but the injured party was, a party; Lord Denning wanted to *bind* the injured party by the terms of a contract to which that party was not, but the wrongdoer was, a party.

(i) *Implied Contract*

Some years before the *Midland Silicones* case, Devlin J had suggested various ways of plugging the gap in a case again involving the Hague Rules, *Pyrene v Scindia Navigation*.[128] A consignment of goods had been sold to the Government of India for shipment from London. All the contractual

---

[124] Perhaps it could be argued that in the case put it would not be fair, just, and reasonable to hold the carrier liable in tort to the cargo-owner. The somewhat remote analogy of *Marc Rich Co AG v Bishop Rock Machine Co Ltd (The Nicholas H)* [1996] AC 211 might be invoked in support of such an argument.

[125] [1962] AC 446, 491.   [126] Ibid.

[127] [1923] KB 420, 441.

[128] *Pyrene Co Ltd v Scindia Navigation Co Ltd* [1954] 2 QB 402.

arrangements for the carriage of the goods had been made by the buyer's agents so that the contract of carriage was between buyer and carriers. One of the items sold, a fire tender, was damaged in the process of being loaded while it was still in the ownership and at the risk of the sellers, who brought an action against the carriers for the cost of repairing it. The carriers argued that their liability was limited by the Hague Rules, which were incorporated in the contract of carriage; and that argument was accepted by Devlin J, who gave three grounds for holding the sellers bound by the limitation of liability in the contract of carriage even though they were not, at least *ex facie*, parties to that contract. The one that he preferred was that a third party 'takes those benefits of the contract which appertain to his interest therein, but takes them, of course, subject to whatever qualifications with regard to them which the contract imposes'.[129] There is something slightly odd about the use of this line of reasoning in the context. One could see the force of it if the sellers had been trying to enforce the contract of carriage. But that was not what they were doing at all; they sought to disregard it. The argument is that the sellers might or could have enforced the contract; therefore they were bound by at least some of its terms. The first limb of the argument was, moreover, based on the doubts as to the existence of the doctrine of privity which had been expressed in earlier cases by Denning LJ;[130] and when these doubts were rejected by the House of Lords in the *Midland Silicones* case,[131] this part of the reasoning of the *Pyrene* case was likewise rejected. That left two further grounds given by Devlin J, for neither of which he had much enthusiasm: that the buyer had acted (at least to some extent) as the sellers' agent in making the contract with the carrier; and that an implied contract incorporating the exemptions and limitations of the main contract of carriage had arisen when the sellers presented the fire tender for loading and the carriers

---

[129] [1954] 2 QB 402, 426.
[130] See the reference in [1954] 2 QB 402, 422 to *Smith and Snipes Hall Farm v River Douglas Catchment Board* [1949] 2 KB 500.
[131] [1926] AC 446; *ante*, p 59.

began to lift it on board. It was the second (implied contract) explanation of the *Pyrene* case which was adopted in the *Midland Silicones* case[132] as the ground on which the *Pyrene* case must now be justified. It is of somewhat limited application in that 'implied contract' reasoning requires some kind of direct contact or dealing between the party claiming the protection of the contract and the third party who is alleged to be bound by its terms.

(ii) *Sub-Bailment on Terms*

So lawyers began to look for another, more promising, exception to the general rule, and the one that they hit upon was bailment, or sub-bailment, on terms. This was seen as a sort of magic wand that was to get rid of any difficulties caused by awkward rules of contract law. I am tempted to adapt Alexander Pope's famous epitaph on Newton:

> God said, *let bailment be!* and all was light.

The starting point for discussing the 'bailment' exception is a passage in the judgment of Lord Denning MR in *Morris v CW Martin Ltd*[133] where a mink stole had been taken to a furrier ('the bailee') for cleaning and had then, with the consent of the owner ('the bailor'), been sent on to a cleaner ('the sub-bailee') who was to do the work under a contract between the furrier and the cleaner. This contract contained exemption clauses which, on their true construction, were held *not* to exclude the cleaner's liability to the owner for loss of the stole by theft. But if the clauses *had* covered that liability, then in Lord Denning's view they could have been relied on by the cleaner against the owner even though they were contained in a contract to which the owner was not a party. 'The owner', he said, 'is bound by the conditions [in the contract between the bailee and the sub-bailee] if he has expressly or impliedly consented to the bailee making a sub-bailment containing those conditions, but not otherwise.'[134] In the context of a discussion of what I have called the twentieth century 'battle over privity' there are six

---

[132] Ibid 471; and see the judgment of Diplock J in that case: [1959] 1 QB 171, 193.
[133] [1966] 1 QB 716.　　　　　　　　　　　　　　　　[134] Ibid 729.

points to be made about this statement.

First, the statement is very close to the ground for Lord Denning's dissent in the *Midland Silicones* case, where he had said: 'when the owner of goods allows the person in possession of them [the bailee] to make a contract in regard to them, then he cannot go back on the terms of the contract, if they are such as he expressly or impliedly authorised, that is to say, consented to be made, even though he was no party to the contract'.[135] The only difference between the two statements relates to the status of the subcontractor: if he is a sub-bailee, he falls within the *Morris v Martin* formula; Lord Denning's *Midland Silicones* formula extends to subcontractors who are not sub-bailees. It would in his view have allowed the stevedores to rely on their contract with the carrier against the cargo-owners even though the stevedores were not bailees of any kind.[136] But of course we have to remember that the majority rejected that view and held that the cargo-owners' claim was not affected by the contract between carriers and stevedores, even though the owner had made a bailment of the goods to the carriers.

Secondly, although Lord Denning's statement in the *Midland Silicones* case was a lone dissent (which is not even mentioned by Lord Brandon in *The Aliakmon*), his statement in *Morris v Martin* has enjoyed wide, and one might almost say enthusiastic, support, most notably in *The Pioneer Container*[137] where it was applied by the Privy Council. At one stage in the development of this subject it was even suggested that the consent of the owner (or bailor) to the terms of the sub-bailment was *not* a necessary condition of the owner's being bound;[138] but that extension of the principle was rejected in *The Pioneer Container*. So we can say that the *Morris v Martin* statement has become the modern orthodoxy: where there is a relationship of bailor, bailee,

---

[135] [1962] AC 446, 491.   [136] pp 59–60 *ante*.

[137] [1994] 2 AC 324; cf also *Compania Portorafti Commerciale SA v Ultramar Panama Inc (The Captain Gregos) (No 2)* [1990] 2 Lloyd's Rep 395, 405.

[138] *Johnson Matthey & Co v Constantine Terminals Ltd* [1976] 2 Lloyd's Rep 215, 221.

and sub-bailee, the bailor is bound by terms of the sub-bailment to which he has expressly or impliedly consented, even though he is not a party to it.

Thirdly, all this has nothing whatsoever to do with the law relating to third party beneficiaries: the term on which the sub-bailee relies is contained in a contract to which he *is* a party. This point is obscured by the invocation in *Morris v Martin*[139] (and in later cases of the present kind[140]) of Lord Sumner's phrase 'bailment on terms' in the *Elder Dempster* case. No doubt it is easy to move from this phrase to 'sub-bailment containing . . . conditions' in *Morris v Martin*. The *Elder Dempster* case did raise a third party beneficiary problem: could the shipowner take the *benefit* of the contract between charterer and cargo-owner. In *Morris v Martin* no attempt was made by the cleaner to rely on any term in the contract between the owner of the stole and the furrier: the question was whether the owner was *bound* by terms in the contract to which he was not a party.

Fourthly, there is the question of the rationale of the 'sub-bailment on terms' exception. Let us suppose for the moment (I shall come back to this question) that the *Midland Silicones* case is right in deciding that the stevedores could not rely on their own contract with the carriers because they were not bailees of the goods;[141] or let us suppose that in *Adler v Dickson*[142] the crew's employment contracts had provided that the crew were to have the same protection as their employers. In the first case, the stevedores could not invoke the *Morris v Martin* principle because though the carriers were bailees, the stevedores were not sub-bailees; in the second, the principle could not apply because carriage of passengers gives rise to no bailment relationship at all (except in relation to their luggage, a point of no relevance to the case). And, even where the wrongdoer is a sub-bailee, he cannot invoke the principle against a person who is not the bailor. This was the reason

---

[139] [1966] 1 QB 716, 730.
[140] eg in *The Pioneer Container* [1994] 2 AC 324, 339.
[141] pp 59–60 *ante*.
[142] [1955] 1 QB 158 (p 56 *ante*).

why the carrier in *The Aliakmon*[143] could not rely on the principle: the bailor in that case was the seller and not the buyer.[144] (In the *Midland Silicones* case[145] the point that the bailment to the carrier was not by the consignee, who made the claim, but by the shipper was not argued.) So the assumption in *The Aliakmon* is that the sub-bailment exception applies only where the injured party is the bailor and the wrongdoer is the sub-bailee: the sub-bailee can then rely on terms in his contract with the intermediate bailee against the bailor, even though there is no contract between bailor and sub-bailee. What is it that sets this situation apart from the others, such as those in *The Aliakmon* and the *Midland Silicones* case (to which the *Morris v Martin* principle does not apply)? The answer seems to be that in the situation in which there is a bailment by the injured party followed by a sub-bailment to which that party has consented, there the injured party may rely, and base his claim, on the very relationship of head bailor and sub-bailee between himself and the wrongdoer as the sole source of the duty alleged to be owed to him by the sub-bailee; and that it is this duty which is excluded or limited by the injured party's consent to the relevant terms of the sub-bailment.[146] But if that is the answer, then the further question arises: why is it that the injured party's consent to such terms suffices only where the relationship in which the terms are contained is a sub-bailment? What is it that is special about bailment? Of course to rely on bailment is a convenient way of saying that you do not need to rely on contract; but that is now true of many other relationships that do not depend on contract but are nevertheless recognized by law as giving rise to a relationship in which there is a duty of care. Is the emphasis on bailment simply an accident of history or termin-

---

[143] [1986] AC 785. There was no reference in Lord Brandon's speech to *Morris v Martin*.

[144] Ibid 818. For the difficulties arising from an apparently contrary obiter dictum in *Borealis AB v Stargas Ltd (The Berge Sisar)* [2001] 2 All ER 193, [2001] UKHL 17 at [18] see *Carver on Bills of Lading* (1st edn, 2001) §7-038 n 47.

[145] [1962] AC 446 (p 60 *ante*).

[146] See *The Pioneer Container* [1994] 2 AC 324, 341.

ology? That is, has it come about simply because bailment is a long-established type of relationship with a convenient label that makes it easy to escape from awkward principles of contract law?

That leads to my fifth point about the *Morris v Martin* principle: what is its scope? Two related questions arise: first, is the relationship of bailor, bailee, and sub-bailee a sufficient, and secondly is it a necessary, condition for the application of the principle? To answer the first question, a distinction must be drawn between, on the one hand, cases in which the sub-bailment is the sole source of the duty alleged to have been broken: eg where the sub-bailee is guilty of a breach of his *custodial* duty so that the goods are lost, whether by misdelivery or otherwise; and, on the other hand, cases in which the sub-bailee damages the goods by negligent conduct and incurs liability, not because he is a bailee, but 'simply by virtue of [his] proximity to the goods'.[147] In the *Johnson Matthey* case,[148] Donaldson J tentatively suggested that in a case of the latter kind the head bailor might not be bound by the terms of a sub-bailment to which he was not a party since he has a cause of action independent of any bailment. So far as my second question is concerned, most of the authorities assume that the existence of a bailment relationship between the injured party and the wrongdoer *is* a necessary condition for the application of the *Morris v Martin* principle. The reasoning of *The Pioneer Container*[149] is based on such a relationship, as is the discussion of the topic in *The Mahkutai*,[150] though there the actual question was whether the sub-bailee could take the *benefit* of the contract between head bailor and original bailee. One could explain the *Midland Silicones*[151] case on the ground that there was no bailment relationship between the relevant parties (the stevedore and the cargo-owner), though that was certainly not the reason given for this aspect of the decision, and the explanation would have an

---

[147] *Hispanica de Petroleos SA v Vencedora Oceanica Navigation SA (The Kapetan Markos NL) (No 2)* [1987] 2 Lloyd's Rep. 321, 340.
[148] [1976] 2 Lloyd's Rep 321, 340.   [149] n 146 *supra*.
[150] [1996] AC 650.   [151] n 145 *supra*.

anachronistic flavour as the *Morris v Martin* principle post-dates the *Midland Silicones* case. But there is also some support for the view that bailment is not a necessary condition for the application of the principle, or at least of a similar principle. This comes from a dictum of Lord Goff in *Henderson v Merrett Syndicates*[152] where he discusses the situation in which there is no bailment but the relationship of the three parties is that of building owner, contractor, and subcontractor. The subcontractor (it is said) 'may be protected from liability by a contractual exemption clause [apparently in the subcontract] authorised by the building owner'. The suggestion is tentative ('may be protected'), and is not easy to fit in with the emphasis on bailment in the authorities to which I have just referred or with the outcome in the *Midland Silicones* case. Perhaps that case could now be explained on the ground that the cargo-owner had *not* authorized the terms of the stevedoring contract (of which he was unaware), but he must have realized that the carrier would be likely to employ subcontractors to unload the ship and have at least by implication consented to their being employed. Or perhaps 'authorized' in the building contract example carries overtones of agency and suggests the creation of a direct collateral contract between building owner and subcontractor. And, apart from authority, there is, with respect, much to be said for Lord Goff's suggestion. The aspect of the privity doctrine which says that a contract does not *bind* a third party is based on the idea that obligations should not be imposed on a person without his consent. The hypothesis in Lord Goff's example is that the third party *has* consented to the term in the subcontract; and while there are no doubt difficulties in enforcing against him a term in a contract to which he is not a party which requires him to *do* something (eg to pay a bonus to the subcontractor), there is not the same degree of difficulty in holding him bound by a term which merely restricts his rights against the subcontractor. For this purpose, it seems that the third party's consent is a

---

[152] [1995] 2 AC 145, 196.

more significant factor than the existence, in addition, of a sub-bailment relationship.

That brings me to the sixth and last question: can the third party be 'bound' by an exemption clause where there is not only no bailment but no consent by the third party? A dictum, again from Lord Goff, in the disappointed beneficiary case of *White v Jones* suggests that even such consent may not invariably be necessary: the solicitor's liability to the beneficiary is said to be 'subject to any term of the contract between the solicitor and the testator which may exclude or restrict the solicitor's liability to the testator'.[153] Normally, the beneficiary will have no knowledge of those terms and may not even know at any relevant time of the existence of the solicitor–client relationship. For this reason, it is perhaps not surprising that there is no support for the suggestion in any of the other speeches in *White v Jones*. But the suggestion may be linked to another, analogous to Lord Roskill's dictum in the *Junior Books* case:[154] namely that a relevant term in the *sub*contract (not, as in that dictum, in the *main* contract) may, by defining what the subcontractor is required to do, adversely affect the party to the main contract who is not in any contractual relations with the subcontractor. This could, for example, have been the position if, in the *Midland Silicones* case, the stevedoring contract had permitted the use of lifting tackle which was not suitable for handling drums of silicones and loss to the cargo-owner had resulted from the use of such equipment. Could the stevedore say that he was not liable to the cargo-owner because he had duly performed all that he had in his contract with the carrier undertaken to do? The law is here in a dilemma. On the one hand (as Bingham LJ has said in discussing an analogous situation[155]) to allow the stevedore to rely on such term in a tort action by the cargo-owner 'could be unfair to him' (the cargo-owner) if he was not aware of (and had not consented to) the terms of the

---

[153] [1995] 2 AC 207, 268.
[154] [1983] AC 520, 546 (p 69 *ante*).
[155] *Simaan General Contracting Co v Pilkington Glass Ltd (No 2)* [1988] QB 758, 782–783.

contract between stevedore and carrier. On the other hand, it would 'make a mockery of the contractual negotiations' between these parties to allow the cargo-owner to sue the stevedore for failing to do something that he had never promised to do. In the example that I have given, I am inclined to come down on the side of the stevedore as he has fully performed his side of the only bargain he has made and to console the third party (the cargo-owner) by pointing out that the carrier is not absolved from contractual liability to him merely because he has, and must be taken to have been authorized to have, employed a subcontractor to perform part of the service that he (the carrier) had contracted to perform.[156] That, of course, leaves the cargo-owner's claim subject to the exemptions and limitations of the contract of carriage; but I see nothing wrong with such an outcome where the tripartite structure is such that the subcontractor is not a wrongdoer.

6. BESWICK V BESWICK

By the time we get to *Beswick v Beswick*,[157] Lord Haldane's 'fundamental' principle[158] of privity had been reasserted in the *Midland Silicones* case;[159] but if there is a moral to be drawn from *Beswick v Beswick* it is how easy it would have been in that case to have avoided or outflanked the operation of the privity doctrine. The facts are well known and simple; but in this age of spin, and also for the sake of playing some variations on them, I shall begin by restating them.

(a) Facts and Result

Peter Beswick was a coal merchant; he had no business premises but only a lorry, some scales, weights and other

---

[156] Cf *Stewart v Reavell's Garage* [1952] QB 545.
[157] [1968] AC 58.
[158] *Dunlop Pneumatic Tyre Co Ltd v Selfridge & Co Ltd* [1915] AC 847, 853.
[159] [1962] AC 446.

utensils. He was over 70 and is accordingly described as 'old Peter Beswick'[160] by Lord Denning MR (who was 67 when the case came before the Court of Appeal) and as 'somewhat elderly'[161] by Danckwerts LJ (who was 78 at the time). Peter was in poor health, having had a leg amputated, and so he decided to retire and to make provision for himself and his wife, Ruth, should she survive him, out of the business. So on 14 March 1962 Peter and his nephew John (who had been helping him with the business) went to see a solicitor, who there and then wrote out an agreement between them which was executed by being signed over a 6d. stamp. Under the agreement, Peter transferred the goodwill of the business (and the lorry and the utensils) to John, who agreed in return to employ Peter as consultant at a weekly salary of £6 10s. for the rest of Peter's life. John further agreed in the event of Peter's death to pay 'the transferor's widow' an annuity 'to be charged on the said business' at the rate of £5 per week; and John also agreed to take over Peter's liability to a number of Peter's creditors: George and Lydia Turner in the sum of £187 and Joseph Beswick in the sum of £250 'or such lesser sum as shall be agreed with the said creditors'. The reports do not tell us what happened to this part of the agreement. The agreement was between Peter and John only; neither Ruth nor any of the named creditors were parties to it. Peter died on 3 November 1963, still married to Ruth, who at this time was 74 and (we are told) in failing health though the ensuing litigation showed that she had plenty of fight left in her. On the day of Peter's funeral John left £5 at Ruth's house, but he made no further payments to Ruth under the agreement. Peter had made no will and Ruth obtained letters of administration to his estate which was valued at a nominal £50: that is, he had 'died without any assets save and except the agreement which he hoped would keep him and then his widow for their lives'.[162] Ruth brought an action against John suing both as Peter's administratrix and in her personal capacity. She claimed (i) £175 arrears of annuity,

---

[160] [1966] Ch 538, 549.   [161] Ibid 558.   [162] [1968] AC 58, 102.

(ii) specific performance of the agreement between Peter and John and an order for payment of annuity (including arrears) due under the agreement, and (iii) declarations that John was liable to her (either personally or as administratrix) to make the payments to her and that they were to be charged on the business. At first instance Burgess VC in the Lancaster Chancery Court dismissed her claims.[163] In the Court of Appeal[164] Lord Denning MR upheld her claims on three grounds: (1) that she could sue at common law in her personal capacity; (2) that she could sue under section 56(1) of the Law of Property Act 1925 in her personal capacity; and (3) that she could in her capacity as administratrix (ie as representing Peter) obtain specific performance of the agreement against John. Danckwerts LJ reached the same conclusion but on a narrower basis, holding that Ruth could sue in her personal capacity under section 56(1) (though not at common law) and that she could obtain specific performance in her capacity as administratrix; and Salmon LJ decided in her favour on the last ground only, ie that, as Peter's administratrix, Ruth could get an order of specific performance. The House of Lords affirmed the decision of the Court of Appeal on the ground given by Salmon LJ, rejected the argument based on section 56(1) of the Law of Property Act, and did not find it necessary to express a concluded view on the question whether Ruth had a right of action in her personal capacity at common law, though the speeches seem to assume that she had no such right.[165]

(b) Ways round Privity

Before we go into the issues raised by the case, let us spare a thought for the solicitor who was asked to draw up the agreement, evidently in something of a hurry. 'The matter', we are told, 'was seemingly urgent and Mr Ashcroft [the solicitor] there and then wrote out an agreement embody-

---

[163] [1965] 3 All ER 858.   [164] [1966] Ch 538.
[165] See [1968] AC 58, 72, 81, 83, 92–93, 95.

ing the terms and it was executed.'[166] Perhaps John was afraid that Peter would not last long and wanted the transfer of the business to be made quickly. If there had been more time for reflection, it would have been relatively easy for the solicitor so to have drafted the agreement as to avoid the impact of the doctrine of privity and so to have saved the legal aid fund[167] the very considerable expense of litigation over relatively small sums. Unless otherwise instructed (a point to which I shall return) the solicitor could have done one of a number of things.

First, he could have made Ruth a party to the contract, that is, he could have included in the agreement a promise by John to Ruth to pay her the £5 per week. That would have given rise to the obvious difficulty that Ruth provided no consideration for John's hypothetical promise to her, but there would have been two easy ways round that difficulty. The first would have been to put the agreement under seal. That would not have been much more difficult than the procedure in fact adopted, of signing the agreement over a 6d. stamp. The procedure for executing a document as a deed would now be even simpler: all that is necessary is the use of words such as 'signed as a deed' and an attesting witness[168] (easily available in a solicitor's office). Such a contract under seal (or now in a deed) would have given Ruth a right to sue on the contract in her personal capacity at common law. It would not, indeed, in her personal capacity have given her any right to specific performance (since equity will not 'aid a volunteer');[169] but this would have been a matter of little or no importance if she had a right at common law to enforce the agreement. If the equitable remedy were the more convenient one (because it would avoid the need for repeated recourse to the court) it could still be sought by Ruth in her capacity as administratrix.

The second way round the difficulty that there was no

---

[166] [1965] 2 All ER 858, 860. When he drew up the agreement on 14 Mar 1962, the solicitor would not have been able to take advantage of the flood of new light that was to be shed on the subject later that year.   [167] See [1966] Ch 538, 567.

[168] Law of Property (Miscellaneous Provisions) Act 1989, s 1.

[169] *Jefferys v Jefferys* (1841) Cr & Ph 138.

consideration moving from Ruth for any promise to her by John would have been to draft the promise as one made jointly to Peter and Ruth. If a promise is made to two persons jointly, it can be enforced by both of them even though the consideration moved from only one of them;[170] indeed, both must be joined as parties to the action.[171] Moreover, on the death of one joint promisee the rights of the deceased promisee pass to the other under the doctrine of survivorship.[172] So if John's promise in *Beswick v Beswick* had been drawn up in this way, then on Peter's death his rights under the supposed promise would have passed to Ruth so that she could have sued on it even though she had not provided any consideration for it.

As an alternative to making Ruth a party to the agreement, the solicitor could have drawn the agreement between Peter and John so as to give rights to Ruth under one of the exceptions to the doctrine of privity of contract. In particular, he might have made use of the exception under which the third party gets enforceable rights because the promisee has constituted himself as trustee of the benefit of the promise for the third party. Reference has already been made to that exception, and the tendency in mid-twentieth century cases has been to narrow its scope by strict insistence on the requirement that the promisee must intend to create a trust in the third party's favour.[173] But that judicial reluctance to apply the exception can be overcome by an express provision in the contract that the promise is taken by the promisee as trustee for the third party. So in *Beswick v Beswick* John's promise to Peter to pay the annuity to Ruth could have been made to Peter expressly as trustee for Ruth. She could then have sued John on the promise even if she had not been Peter's administratrix: eg if Peter had made a will appointing his hypothetical brother Paul as executor. An action on the promise could then have been brought by Ruth against

---

[170] See *Coulls v Bagot's Executor and Trusted Co Ltd* (1967) 119 CLR 60.
[171] *Sorsbie v Park* (1843) 12 M & W 146.
[172] *Anderson v Martindale* (1801) 1 East 497.
[173] *Re Schebsman* [1944] Ch 83 (p 52 *ante*).

John, joining 'Paul' as a party to the action.

If, then, it would have been so easy for the solicitor to have drawn up the agreement so as to confer enforceable rights on Ruth, why did he not do so? The reports do not provide any answer to this question and there seem to be two possibilities. One is that the agreement was drawn up in haste, evidently imposed by Peter and John on their solicitor. But I am reluctant to impute negligence to the solicitor and the other possibility is that he was simply carrying out his instructions. We have no way of knowing what passed between him and his clients on 14 March 1962; but there is the possibility of his having told Peter and John (1) that they could create legally enforceable rights in favour of Ruth but (2) that if they did so, their right to vary their contract would be lost or limited. Peter and John might not have liked that idea and instructed him accordingly. I make these points because of their relevance to the case for reform and to the scope of that reform when it was finally achieved; I shall return to this aspect of the case in my discussion of the latter topic. For the moment I want to concentrate on the common law position, using that expression here to include equity but to exclude statute.

That common law position can be summed up in three propositions. First, the third party (Ruth in her personal capacity) has no cause of action against the promisor (John) in contract. Secondly, the promisee (Ruth in her representative capacity) does have a remedy by way of specific performance against the promisor. Thirdly, one reason for granting the equitable remedy of specific performance was thought to be that the promisee's common law remedy was inadequate because no loss had been suffered by the estate so that, in the view of the majority of the House of Lords, the estate could recover no more than nominal damages (£2 had in fact been paid into court on John's behalf). This is a version of the 'legal black hole'[174] argument found in later cases: the business had been transferred to John and he should not be allowed to get away with refusing to perform

---

[174] See n 19 *supra.*

his counter-promise. The hole is not totally black (if such a solecism may be forgiven) as John had made the payments promised to Peter and one to Ruth, and may have paid off the creditors; on the other hand, he was *deliberately* refusing to perform his promise to Ruth and in this respect his conduct is worse than the negligence of the defendants in the other cases in which the courts have been afraid of creating such 'black holes'. Setting these points aside, the question to be discussed here is how far, if at all, the fear of a 'black hole' in *Beswick v Beswick* may be allayed by later common law developments. The question subdivides into two. Could Ruth now improve her chances by suing anyone in tort? And what is the effect on the reasoning of *Beswick v Beswick* of later developments in the law relating to damages in respect of a third party's loss?

(c) Tort Liability?

So far as liability in tort is concerned, the most obvious target of such a claim would be the solicitor who drew up the agreement and who could without too much difficulty have drawn it up so as to confer an enforceable right on Ruth in her personal capacity. I have suggested that there are two possible reasons why he did not do so. One was that he was in this respect carrying out Peter's and John's instructions and, if that was the case, then he would not owe any duty of care to Ruth. The other is that he was negligent (and I emphasize that I do not say that he was). But if that was the position then it is at least prima facie arguable that he did owe a duty of care to Ruth on the principle of the disappointed beneficiary cases such as *White v Jones*.[175] Recent cases such as *Gorham v British Telecommunications plc*[176] show that this principle is not restricted to testamentary beneficiaries; and in one respect at least this aspect of *Beswick v Beswick* comes very close to *Gorham's* case: one of Peter's purposes in entering into the agreement was to make provision for his widow. So it is certainly arguable

---

[175] [1995] 2 AC 207.   [176] [2000] 1 WLR 2129.

that the solicitor owed Ruth a duty of care; but there is also the counter-argument, based on other disappointed beneficiary cases,[177] that no such duty is owed if, when the defect in the will is discovered, matters can still be put right. In *Beswick v Beswick* it was possible to put matters right when the 'defect' in the contract was discovered and they were in fact put right when the order of specific performance was obtained. The result of that order, moreover, was that even if a duty of care was owed to Ruth by the solicitor, she suffered no loss in consequence of its breach. So to make this issue come alive we have to imagine that John's promise was of a kind that was *not* specifically enforceable: eg that the promise had been to mow Ruth's lawn once a week during the months of April to October. I shall assume that the promise was one by John to do the work personally, and not merely to procure it to be done, so that specific performance of it would not have been available.[178] In that case the possibility of making the solicitor liable in tort grows stronger, though it is subject to the possibility to be discussed below of a satisfactory remedy in damages being available to the estate. Before discussing that question, I should perhaps say that I see no possibility of Ruth's having a remedy in tort against John for his refusal to perform his contract with Peter. To allow a tort remedy against the promisor in such a situation would amount to giving damages for loss of an expectation having no existence apart from the promise which gave rise to it; it would mean that any contract by which A promised B to pay money to C would give C a remedy in tort against A and that the common law doctrine of privity would cease to exist, quite apart from statute. So far, at least, the courts have refused to go this far;[179] and their reluctance to do so is further supported by the generally hostile reception which has been given to the *Junior Books* case.[180]

---

[177] *Hemmens v Wilson Browne* [1995] Ch 223; *Walker v Medlicott* [1999] 1 WLR 727.

[178] See eg *Johnson v Shrewsbury & Birmingham Railway* (1853) 3 DM & G 358.

[179] *Balsamo v Medici* [1984] 1 WLR 951.

[180] [1983] 1 AC 520; Treitel, *The Law of Contract* (10th edn, 1999) 562–563.

(*d*) **Damages in Respect of Third Party's Loss**

The second of my two questions concerns the effect on the reasoning of *Beswick v Beswick* of later developments in the law relating to damages in respect of a third party's loss; at the time of the decision, all the significant twentieth century discussions of this topic still lay in the future. In holding that specific performance was available, the majority of the House of Lords took the view that damages were an inadequate remedy since they would be no more than nominal. The reason for this view is that, in Lord Upjohn's words, Peter had 'died without any assets save and except the agreement which he hoped would keep him and then his widow for their lives'.[181] He appears here to have in mind damages in respect of loss suffered *by the estate*: ie the point that, on John's default, there was no money in the estate to make alternative provision for Ruth, and so the estate could not have incurred the cost of making any such provision. Lord Pearce, alone, thought that 'the damages, if assessed, must be substantial'[182] and it is not entirely clear from this part of his speech whether the remedy that he had in mind was indeed one by way of damages, as opposed to one for the promised sum.[183] Whether the promisee can sue for the sum which the promisor promised to pay to the third party remains a controversial point; probably he can do so only if the promise is one to pay the third party or as the promisee shall direct.[184] But assuming that Lord Pearce's dicta do refer to damages, the damages that he has in mind appear to be damages recoverable by the estate in respect of the third party's loss. The majority simply assume that such damages are not available and that assumption is no doubt correct as a general rule. That general rule was recognized in *Woodar v Wimpey*[185] where, as in *Beswick v Beswick*, the

---

[181] [1968] AC 68, 102.   [182] Ibid 88.
[183] Cf *infra* at n 193.
[184] See *Tradigrain SA v King Diamond Shipping SA (The Spiros C)* [2000] 2 Lloyd's Rep 319, 331.
[185] *Woodar Investment Development Ltd v Wimpey Construction Co Ltd* [1980] 1 WLR 277: recognition of the rule is implicit in the criticism of it; see *infra* at n 192.

promise was one to pay a sum of money to a third party, though the actual decision was that the promisor was not liable as there had been no wrongful repudiation by him. Even before *Beswick v Beswick* there were exceptions to the general rule, and since that case there has been a considerable development of these exceptions, with the pendulum swinging (as such things are apt to do) in each direction in turn. In particular, one of the exceptions was, in the last quarter of the twentieth century, the subject of a long and complex development, of which no more than a rough sketch can be given here. The exception in question relates to contracts for the carriage of goods by sea, where *The Albazero*[186] recognized that a shipper could recover damages from the carrier in respect of loss suffered, not by the shipper himself, but by the consignee to whom the goods had been sold and to whom risk had passed before the loss or damage resulting from the carrier's breach of his contract with the shipper had occurred. At the same time, the exception was limited by the actual decision in *The Albazero*, which was that the exception did not apply where the consignee had acquired his own contractual rights against the carrier, typically by transfer of the bill of lading. In the *Linden Gardens* case[187] that exception was, in effect, extended to building contracts; and it was then cut off from at least one of its roots in the *Darlington* case[188] where it was applied in spite of the fact that the subject matter of the contract was never transferred to the third party but had belonged to him at all relevant times. That extension was apparently approved by the House of Lords in the *Panatown* case[189] where, however, the majority of the House of Lords reconnected the exception to another of its roots by holding that the exception did not, in a building contract context any more than in the carriage by sea cases, apply

---

[186] *Albacruz (Cargo Owners) v Albazero (Owners) (The Albazero)* [1977] AC 774, recognizing the so-called 'rule in *Dunlop v Lambert*' (1839) 2 Cl & F 626 but not applying it for the reason stated in the text above.

[187] *Linden Gardens Trust v Lenesta Sludge Disposals Ltd* [1994] 1 AC 85.

[188] *Darlington BC v Wiltshier Northern Ltd* [1995] 1 WLR 68.

[189] *Alfred McAlpine Construction Ltd v Panatown Ltd* [2001] 1 AC 518.

where the third party had his own contractual remedy against the contractor whose defective work was the cause of the loss. Fascinating as the conflict of judicial opinion in that case may be, a detailed discussion of it would take me too far from the different kind of problem that arose in *Beswick v Beswick*. The carriage by sea and building cases were all cases of defective performance of services causing the loss of, or damage to, the third party's property. *Beswick v Beswick*, on the other hand, was a case of wrongful failure, or refusal, to perform a simple promise to pay money to the third party. In this respect it resembles the position in *Woodar v Wimpey*[190] as it would there have been if the refusal to pay the third party had been wrongful. It is therefore to that case that we have to look for guidance on the question whether, in the light of later developments, the estate in *Beswick v Beswick* could now recover substantial damages in respect of Ruth's loss. Unfortunately we do not find much guidance since the actual decision in *Woodar v Wimpey* was that there was *no* wrongful repudiation; and the question what the damages would have been if there had been such a repudiation is said to be 'one of great doubt and difficulty'.[191] The assumption seems to be that the promisee can recover damages only in respect of his own loss since it is this assumed position which is said to be 'most unsatisfactory'[192] and to call for reconsideration by the House of Lords or the legislature. What seems to underlie this criticism is the fear of a legal black hole—a danger that was neatly averted in *Beswick v Beswick* by the order of specific performance. Indeed, even Lord Pearce favoured this remedy since it was 'more convenient than an action [by the administratrix] for arrears followed by separate actions as each sum falls due'.[193]

But of course this method of avoiding the legal black hole would not be available if we again varied the facts of *Beswick v Beswick* so that John's promise was one that was *not* specifically enforceable: eg because it was a contract for

[190] n 185 *supra*.   [191] [1980] 1 WLR 277, 284.
[192] Ibid 291.   [193] [1994] 1 AC 85, 87.

personal service, as in my lawnmowing example. That example comes close to the one given by Lord Griffiths in the *Linden Gardens* case of the husband who contracts with a builder to have the roof on his wife's house repaired. But there is this difference: in Lord Griffiths's case, the problem arises because the builder does the work defectively; in my hypothetical case, John simply refuses or fails to cut the grass at all. The building cases (and indeed the carriage by sea cases) are all cases of *defective* performance. The case of simple non-performance did not seem to have troubled Lord Griffiths at all, probably because he assumes that the builder would in such a case not have been paid since in a contract of this kind performance is prima facie a condition precedent to the right to be paid.[194] The husband could then use the money so saved to get the work done by another builder and if that builder charged more than had been promised to the original one, then (subject to possible considerations of mitigation and remoteness) the husband could recover the difference as damages for his *own* (not for the third party's) loss. Similar reasoning would apply if, under the original contract, the builder had been paid in advance and had not done any of the promised work: he would have to return the advance payment; and the husband could then proceed as before. But my hypothetical variation on *Beswick v Beswick* is more complex than either of the two examples just given because John had not only been 'paid' in advance (Peter's business had been transferred to him) but had also partly performed his contract with Peter: he had made the weekly payments to Peter during Peter's life, he had made one payment to Ruth, and he may have paid the creditors. What proportion these acts of part performance bore to the entirety of his obligations under the contract with Peter, it is hard to tell; and in these circumstances there would be, to say the least, difficulty in the way of a restitution claim on behalf of the estate.[195] If

---

[194] *Morton v Lamb* (1797) 7 TR 125; *Miles v Wakefield MDC* [1987] AC 539, 561.

[195] The rationale of the requirement that 'failure of consideration' must be 'total' would seem to apply, however much that requirement may be attenuated where

there is no such claim, then we do seem to have a situation in which there would be at least a partial legal black hole unless the estate could claim damages in respect of Ruth's loss.

(e) Law of Property Act 1925, Section 56(1)

I turn from the common law position in *Beswick v Beswick* to that arising under statute. Two points arise: the first, which is extensively discussed in the case, is whether section 56(1) of the Law of Property Act 1925 applied on the facts; and it is with at least some aspects of this point that I shall deal here. The second is what effect, if any, the Contracts (Rights of Third Parties) Act 1999 would have on facts such as those of *Beswick v Beswick*. I shall come back to this point when discussing legislative reform of the privity doctrine in the final part of this lecture.

It is not easy to retain the attention of an audience while lecturing on section 56(1) of the Law of Property Act 1925. But in *Beswick v Beswick* most of the discussion in the House of Lords is devoted to this topic; and I can only assume that it was the wish to deal with it that induced the House to grant leave to appeal, which had been refused by the Court of Appeal. So far as relevant to our discussion, the subsection provides that 'A person may take . . . the benefit of any . . . covenant or agreement over or respecting land *or other property*, although he may not be named as a party to the conveyance or other instrument.' This must be read together with the definition in the Act of 'property' so as to include (unless the context otherwise requires) 'any thing in action'.[196] In the Court of Appeal, Lord Denning MR and Danckwerts LJ had held that John's promise to pay the annuity was a 'thing in action' and therefore 'property' within section 56(1) and that Ruth could therefore enforce that promise by virtue of the subsection even though she

---

there is no difficulty in apportioning the part left unperformed to the whole of the promised performance: see Treitel, *The Law of Contract* (10th edn, 1999) 978–979.

[196] S 205(1)(xx).

was not 'named as a party' to the contract between Peter and John. In their view, the words of section 56(1) consisted of a 'clear' provision to this effect and had, in the case of written contracts, reversed the rule laid down in *Tweddle v Atkinson*. The House of Lords were unanimous in rejecting this view and in holding that Ruth had no right of action in her personal capacity under section 56(1). So far as the wording of the subsection is concerned, that seems, with respect, to be the preferable view. A draftsman setting out to reverse *Tweddle v Atkinson* would surely not use the convoluted language of section 56(1): in particular, he would not use the phrase 'although he is not *named as a party*' when he meant 'although he *is not* a party'. This point is reflected in the orthodox view which had been established by cases before *Beswick v Beswick*,[197] was approved in that case, and has been followed since then.[198] Under that view, it is essential that the instrument should not merely be capable of benefiting the third party: it must also purport to make a grant to or covenant with him, even though it need not name him.

The members of the House of Lords in *Beswick v Beswick* express a variety of views on the question exactly when section 56(1) *does* apply; but they are unanimous on the point that it does *not* apply to a simple promise by A to B to pay money to C. In reaching this conclusion, the House of Lords relied mainly on the legislative history of section 56(1), emphasizing the then well-known point that the subsection was intended to re-enact, with some extension, an earlier enactment of 1845,[199] but not to revolutionize the law by abolishing the doctrine of privity of contract. In *Beswick v Beswick*, the House of Lords was not allowed to refer for this purpose to the Parliamentary proceedings on the 1925 property legislation; but we can now do so, at least so far as *Pepper v Hart*[200] allows; and what we find in those proceedings is not without interest. Before the passing of

[197] eg *Stromdale and Ball Ltd v Burden* [1952] Ch 223.
[198] eg *Amsprop Trading Ltd v Harris Distribution Ltd* [1997] 1 WLR 1025.
[199] Real Property Act 1845.
[200] [1993] AC 593.

the 1925 Act, a number of reforming bills had been passed, but what is now section 56(1) does not occur in any of them. The reforming Acts were then consolidated, together with earlier legislation, into what we now know as the 1925 property legislation. In introducing one of the reforming bills in the House of Lords, the Lord Chancellor said that, if the reforming bills were passed, no parliamentary time would be needed for the consolidating bills 'because they do not change what will then be the law'.[201] That Lord Chancellor was Lord Haldane, who had in *Dunlop v Selfridge* said that 'In the law of England certain principles are fundamental. One is that only a person who is a party to a contract can sue upon it.'[202] Clearly it cannot have been his view that section 56(1) was intended to reverse that 'fundamental' principle.

The view that section 56(1) did not have any such dramatic effect is also supported by its contemporary reception. There is no reference to the subsection in the first edition of Cheshire's *Modern Real Property* (1925): it receives no mention in that work until the fifth edition (1944). Also significant is the attitude of Sir Benjamin Cherry, who took a considerable part in the drafting of the 1925 property legislation. In the twenty-second edition of Prideaux's *Precedents in Conveyancing* (1926), page 10, he tells us that sections 51–75 of the Law of Property Act 1925 'relate to conveyancing'. He then gives a list of eight 'main points to note'. Section 56(1) is not one of them. Contemporary opinion clearly did not take the view that section 56(1) had abolished the 'fundamental' common law doctrine of privity.

The books on contract were even slower in taking the subsection to heart. There is no reference to section 56(1) in the first edition of *Cheshire & Fifoot* (1945). In that work the subsection makes its first appearance in the fourth edition (1956) and in *Anson* it does not appear until 1959, in the twenty-first edition, the first to be edited by Professor A. G. Guest QC. The fact that the Law Revision Committee had

---

[201] 59 HL Deb, 31 July 1924, col 125.
[202] [1915] AC 847, 853 (p 49 *ante*).

cited the subsection in its Sixth Interim Report in 1937 as
one of the statutory exceptions to the doctrine of privity
seems to have attracted no attention from writers on
contract law at the time.

You may ask: does any of this discussion of section 56(1)
still matter now that we have the Contracts (Right of Third
Parties) Act 1999? The answer is that it still does, for two
related reasons. First, any right of enforcement which a
third party may have under the 1999 Act is subject to the
provisions of that Act while rights under section 56(1) are
not so subject. So if a third party had rights under both
enactments he might prefer to exercise his rights under
section 56(1)[203] so as to escape from the limitations on rights
arising under the 1999 Act. Secondly, a person who had *no*
rights under the 1999 Act[204] might seek to rely instead on
section 56(1); and so the scope of the subsection remains a
live issue even after the movement for reform which culmi-
nated in 1999. It is to that topic that I turn as the concluding
part of this lecture.

(f) Legislative Reform

The outcome of the *Midland Silicones* case and of *Beswick v
Beswick* was that the doctrine of privity survived the direct
frontal attacks that had been launched on it by Lord
Denning. But it did not enjoy a very high popularity rating
with the judiciary. In 1982 Lord Diplock described it as 'an
anachronistic shortcoming that has for many years been
regarded as a reproach to English law';[205] and in 1995 Steyn
LJ said that it was an 'unjust rule' for which there was 'no
doctrinal, logical or policy reason'.[206] The first proposal for
legislative reform in England was made by the Law Revision Committee in 1937, not so much in response to judicial
criticism (which came later) but on the ground that English

---

[203] Such rights would be among those preserved by s 7(1) of the 1999 Act.

[204] eg because he was not 'identified' in accordance with the requirements of
s 1(3) of the 1999 Act.

[205] *Swain v Law Society* [1983] 1 AC 598, 611.

[206] *Darlington BC v Wiltshier Northern Ltd* [1995] 1 WLR 68, 76.

law stood alone in its 'rigid' denial of the existence of a *jus quaesitum tertio*;[207] though, as the Committee then proceeds to list five statutory and one judge-made exception to the English position, the denial is by no means as rigid as the Committee's opening criticism may suggest. One cannot resist the speculation that Professor Goodhart's membership of the Committee and his association (via the Yale Law School) with Corbin may have been at least one historical source of this part of the Report: certainly Corbin's article on third party beneficiaries in the 1930 volume of the *Law Quarterly Review*[208] is cited as a footnote to paragraph 42 of the Report and is the only academic contribution to the subject to be so honoured. Corbin's reasoning in that article is not adopted in the Report; indeed, it would have done away with the need for legislative reform. The main case for such reform seems to have been that the law on trusts of promises was obscure and occasionally caused inconvenience. One may recall with some nostalgia that the part of the Report on third parties occupies less than six octavo pages (as against the 194 pages of A4 in the Law Commission's 1996 Report[209]). The main recommendation in this part of the Report was that 'where a contract by its express terms purports to confer a benefit directly on a third party', the third party should be entitled to enforce the contract 'in his own name' (ie, it seems, without having to join the promisee as a party to the action). This right was to be subject to two qualifications. The first was that the right of enforcement was to be 'subject to any defences that would have been valid between the contracting parties'; the second was that 'unless the contract otherwise provides, it may be cancelled by the mutual consent of the contracting parties at any time before the third party has adopted it either expressly or by conduct'. This proposal was never implemented in England;[210] legislative reform was to be deferred for another sixty-two years. But the very fact that

---

[207] Sixth Interim Report, Cmd 5449 (1937), s D §41.   [208] p 51 *ante.*
[209] *Privity of Contract: Contracts for the Benefit of Third Parties*, Law Com No 242 (1996).
[210] See Beatson, [1992] CLP 1.

the 1937 proposal had been made may have been influential in two respects. First, it may have helped to increase judicial awareness of the need for reform; and secondly the very fact that it was made may have served as a brake on judicial activity in the sense that most judges came to think of radical reform of this branch of the law as a matter for Parliament rather than as one for judicial activity. That is firmly the view of Lord Simonds in the *Midland Silicones* case: 'The law is developed by the application of old principles to new circumstances. Therein lies its genius. Its reform by the abrogation of those principles is the task not of the courts but of Parliament.'[211] Lord Reid is less forthright but is essentially on the same side: 'Although I may regret it, I find it impossible to deny the existence of the general rule that a stranger cannot in a question with either of the contracting parties take advantage of provisions of the contract, even where it is clear from the contract that some provision in it was intended to benefit him.'[212] And his conclusion is that 'I must decide this case on the established principles of the law of England.'[213] By the time we get to *Beswick v Beswick*, indeed, Lord Reid's patience begins to wear rather thin. After referring to the Law Revision Committee's 1937 Report he said: 'If one had to contemplate a further period of Parliamentary procrastination, this House might find it necessary to deal with the matter.'[214] That was said in June 1967, not long after the House of Lords had declared that it had the power to depart from its own decisions.[215] The 'Parliamentary procrastination' was to last for thirty-two more years, during which Lord Reid's threat, or promise, of judicial intervention was from time to time repeated by other members of the House of Lords.[216] Curiously, no such threat or promise was made in relation to the principal part of the 1937 Report, over half of which

---

[211] [1962] AC 446, 468.   [212] Ibid 473.
[213] Ibid 479.   [214] [1968] AC 58, 72.
[215] Practice Statement (Judicial Precedent) [1966] 1 WLR 1234.
[216] eg in *Woodar Investment Development Ltd v Wimpey Construction UK Ltd* [1980] 1 WLR 277, 291, 297–298, 300; *Swain v Law Society* [1983] AC 598, 611; cf also the view of Steyn LJ in the *Darlington* case (n 206 *supra*) [1995] 1 WLR 68, 76.

was devoted to reform of the doctrine of consideration (as against less than a quarter to privity). My view, in agreement with that of the Law Commission, is that the complexities of the subject are such that it was more appropriately the subject of legislative than of judicial reform. I can best illustrate the point by reference to other common law systems, especially to that (or those) of the United States which does (or do) recognize the rights of third party beneficiaries as a matter of common law. The judicially developed third party beneficiaries law has become a subject of awesome complexity. Let me mention just a few of the reasons for this complexity.

First, there is the question just who qualifies as a third party beneficiary. The extremes to which courts have gone are perhaps best illustrated by the American case of *Freer v Putnam Funeral Home* (1937)[217] where a contract between a doctor and his patient contained a promise by the doctor in certain events (which happened) to pay the patient's funeral expenses. Two days after the contract was made the patient died and it was held that the undertaker was entitled to enforce the promise as a third party beneficiary. The case may be extreme, even in the American law of third party beneficiaries, but it does illustrate the dangers in this context of judicial activism free from legislative control.

Secondly, there is the question of the extent to which the acquisition of rights by a third party restricts the rights of the contracting parties to rescind or vary the contract by agreement. Suppose that in *Beswick v Beswick*, before Peter's death, his former coal-selling business had fallen on hard times through no fault of John's, and it had been agreed between them to reduce the weekly payments both to Peter and to Ruth. Under a judge-made system, could they have done so?

Thirdly, there is the question of the extent to which defences between the parties are available against the third party. Suppose that in *Beswick v Beswick* the coal lorry had broken down the day after it had been handed over to John

[217] 111 SW 2d 463 (1937).

and that this had amounted to a repudiatory breach by Peter. Would a court, under a common law doctrine of third party beneficiaries, and without legislative guidance of the kind now provided by section 3 of the Contracts (Rights of Third Parties) Act 1999, have allowed John to rely on that breach as a defence to an action brought by Ruth in her personal capacity under such a doctrine?

Fourthly, we have to look at the effect of the promise, not only between promisor, promisee, and third party, but in a wider context. In a number of the decided cases, the substantial issue has been, not between the third party and the promisor, but between the third party and the promisee's creditors, or his estate: this was true, for example, in *Re Schebsman*.[218] In *Beswick v Beswick*, the contract seems to have disposed, in substance, of all of Peter's assets; and so it raised a problem about the protection of his creditors. The solicitor (or someone) did think of this: the agreement provided that John was to pay off some of Peter's creditors. But what if it had not done so and the real contest had been, not between Ruth and John, but between Ruth and those creditors? Or suppose that the annuity had, under the agreement, been payable not to Ruth but to some other lady with whom Peter had formed a surreptitious liaison. Would this dark lady have engaged as much judicial sympathy as Ruth had done, especially if enforcement of her claim was at Ruth's expense in the sense of giving that other lady a benefit which, had it been conferred by will, could have been open to challenge under the legislation relating to protection for dependants?

All these are difficult problems which in the United States have led to a huge body of case law. The account of it in *Corbin* covers more than 350 pages[219] and the expense of the underlying litigation must have been huge. That is one reason for favouring an orderly solution such as that now contained in the Contracts (Rights of Third Parties) Act 1999. I know that in some branches of the law the courts favour a case by case or incremental approach; but in this

---

[218] [1944] Ch 83.   [219] *Corbin on Contracts* (1951), chs 41–44.

topic a statutory scheme is, in my view, preferable both as promoting clarity and as reducing expense. I know also that the 1999 Act has already generated a very considerable literature (for some of which I have to take responsibility). But that literature, so far, consists entirely of academic speculation. Even at that level, it would be dwarfed by the entirety of academic discussion of the American law and by the vast bulk of primary source material on which that speculation is based.

So far, I have expressed my preference for a legislative solution over what may be called a developed judge-made third party beneficiary doctrine. That preference becomes even stronger when we come to common law systems in which such a doctrine can perhaps be said to be emerging from judicial decisions but to be as yet in an underdeveloped form. The resulting uncertainty in these systems is bewildering. It is almost impossible to extract a *ratio decidendi* from the Australian *Trident Insurance* case,[220] or to say how far the Canadian courts will take the exception to the privity doctrine created in the *London Drugs* case[221] (and now extended in the *Fraser River*[222] case). Again, the legislative solution that we now have in England seems to me to be preferable in avoiding this very high degree of uncertainty. Of course its virtues should not be exaggerated; many difficulties of interpretation remain. But the Act has taken a significant step towards the 'clarity and accessibility'[223] of contract law which were stated by the Law Commission in its very first programme of law reform as objectives of the examination of the law of contract, at that time with a view to its codification.

It would take too long in this lecture to attempt anything like a comprehensive account of the Contracts (Rights of Third Parties) Act 1999 which finally brought legislative reform to this branch of the law. But I do want to touch on

---

[220] *Trident Insurance Co Ltd v McNiece Bros Pty Ltd* (1988) 165 CLR 107.

[221] [1992] 3 SCR 299 (n 55 *supra*).

[222] *Fraser River Pile and Dredge Ltd v Can-Drive Services Ltd* [2000] 1 Lloyd's Rep 199.

[223] First Programme of the Law Commission (1965) Part I.

the question how that Act would affect the outcome on the facts of the two cases with which my discussion of the twentieth century developments has been mainly concerned: the *Midland Silicones* case and *Beswick v Beswick*.

The *Midland Silicones* case, as will be recalled, raised two issues: were the stevedores entitled to the benefit of the contract between cargo-owners and carriers; and were the cargo-owners bound by the contract between stevedores and carriers. The second issue is not affected by the 1999 Act at all. The Act confers *rights* on persons who are not parties to the contract; it does not *bind* such persons by the terms of a contract between others.[224] At most, if they seek to enforce one term of such a contract, they may find that their rights under it are subject to other terms in it;[225] but this was not the position in the *Midland Silicones* case: the cargo-owners were not trying to enforce a contract term against the stevedores. So we come back to the first issue and the answer, fairly clearly, is that this is not affected by the 1999 Act either. A third party's right to enforce a term of a contract arises under section 1(1) only if '(a) the contract expressly provides that he may' or '(b) ... the term purports to confer a benefit on him'; and there is the further requirement in section 1(3) that 'the third party· must be expressly identified in the contract by name, as a member of a class or as answering a particular description'. None of these requirements was satisfied since the contract did not mention the stevedores but limited the liability only of 'the carrier'. On the facts of the *Midland Silicones* case, we would now be in exactly the same legal position as that in which the United States Supreme Court found itself in the *Robert C Herd* case (1959):[226] that is, we now have (within limits) a third party beneficiary doctrine, but the stevedores are not contract beneficiaries. That conclusion is, however, in practical terms not very significant since bills of lading nowadays generally contain Himalaya clauses and the Act

---

[224] Law Commission's Report on *Privity of Contract: Contracts for the Benefit of Third Parties*, Law Com No 242 (1996) §§10.32, 7.6.

[225] 1999 Act, ss 1(4) and 3; cf Law Com No 242 (n 224 *supra*) §10.24.

[226] 359 US 297 (1959) (pp 62–63, 65–66 *ante*).

provides that, where a contract term 'excludes or limits' liability, references in the Act to a third party's 'enforcing' the term are to be 'construed as references to his availing himself of the exclusion or limitation'.[227] So if the bill of lading now contained a Himalaya clause, the stevedores would under the Act be entitled to avail themselves of the limitation of liability term in the bill of lading. But they would be able to do so on quite a different theory from that underlying the enforceability of Himalaya clauses at common law. The common law theory is that the clause, together with the conduct of the parties, brings into existence a direct contract between stevedore and cargo-owner; the theory of the Act is that the stevedore acquires rights of 'enforcement' as a third party beneficiary to a contract to which he is *not* a party. The third party's rights under the Act are, moreover, subject to its provisions (as section 1(1) provides), while common law rights acquired by virtue of Himalaya clauses are not; and if the third party for some reason prefers to rely on rights or defences 'available apart from [the] Act', then section 7(1) provides that he may do so. For this reason, among others, it would not be safe to jettison all the old learning about Himalaya clauses and to rely entirely on the simpler forms of words that would protect third parties under the Act.

As for *Beswick v Beswick*, the Law Commission, in its Report which led to the passing of the 1999 Act, say that they think that Ruth 'would have the right of enforcement'[228] under the Act, but I am not so sure. The contract between Peter and John did not expressly provide that Ruth was to have the right to enforce any term of that contract, so that section 1(1)(a) would not be satisfied; but the term under which John was to pay her £5 a week no doubt purported to confer a benefit on her so that prima facie she would have such a right under section 1(1)(b). But this provision is stated in section 1(2) not to apply 'if on a proper construction of the contract it appears that the parties did not intend the term to be enforceable by the third party'. So

---

[227] S 1(6).   [228] (n 224 *supra*), §7.46.

the question arises as to whether Peter and John 'did not intend the term to be enforceable by' Ruth; and under the rules relating to the admissibility of extrinsic evidence as an aid to construction it seems that evidence of what Peter and John intended would be admissible on this issue since the subsection expressly refers to their intention. We of course do not know what they intended; the facts which are now relevant to this issue were not established since, under the law as it then stood, they were irrelevant. We come back to the question: what was said in the solicitor's office before the contract between Peter and John was made? If they did intend Ruth to have an enforceable right, the solicitor could easily have drawn up the agreement so as to confer one on her. Why did he not do so? Was it because he did not have enough time to think about the relevant law, or because he was following his instructions? I shall leave it there, on the principle that it is always safer to end a discussion with a question than with an attempt to provide an answer.

3

Types of Contractual Terms

I shall start with the no doubt provocative statement that we began the twentieth century with a division of contractual terms into two classes and ended it with four.

1. CONDITIONS AND WARRANTIES

The division into two classes and the terminology relating to it of course go back to the Sale of Goods Act 1893 and are retained, so far as English law is concerned, in the present 1979 version of the Act, as subsequently amended. There, the distinction is drawn between 'conditions' and 'warranties', the purpose of the distinction being to tell us whether a buyer to whom non-conforming goods are tendered or delivered is entitled to reject them: that is, to refuse to take delivery or, if the goods have been delivered, to return them and (in either case) to refuse to pay for them, or, if he has paid, to get his money back against return of the goods. These are remedies for *undoing* rather than for *enforcing* the contract. Similar remedies of refusing to accept performance, refusing to perform, and claiming restitution are available in relation to contracts other than those for the sale of goods. It will be convenient to refer to this bundle of remedies as rescission of the contract for breach. The use of the word 'rescission' in this context has been the subject of judicial criticism[1] but the usage continues to be found in the judicial opinions even of its critics[2] and there is no harm in it so long as we bear in mind, as Lord Diplock has urged us to do,[3] that such 'rescission' does not deprive the injured

---

[1] eg *Photo Production Ltd v Securicor Transport Ltd* [1980] AC 827, 844 (*per* Lord Wilberforce).

[2] eg *Gill & Duffus SA v Berger Co Inc* [1984] AC 382, 390, 393 (*per* Lord Diplock).

[3] *Photo Production case* (n 1 *supra*) 851.

party of his right to damages in respect of the breach. I am content with the high authority of Devlin J: 'the right to reject is merely a particular form of the right to rescind'.[4] The legal background to the discussion that follows is that, as a general rule, the injured party can rescind for breach only if he can show that the breach has caused him *serious* prejudice;[5] but this general rule is subject to many exceptions,[6] one of which comes into operation when the breach is one of a 'condition' of the contract.

The Sale of Goods Act defines 'warranty' as an agreement with reference to the goods sold which is 'collateral to the main purpose of' the contract, 'the breach of which gives rise to a claim for damages but not to a right to reject the goods';[7] the Act does not define 'condition' but makes it clear[8] that this means a term the breach of which does give rise to a right to reject (or simply to refuse to accept and pay). The Act uses the distinction only in relation to breach by the *seller*: it does not use it in relation to breach by the buyer, though it has been used in this context by the courts.[9] The Act does say that stipulations as to the time of payment are prima facie not of the essence of the contract,[10] which makes them in some ways look like warranties; but this appearance is slightly deceptive in the light of the unpaid seller's right of resale (as defined by the Act),[11] the exercise of which is said to 'rescind' the contract.[12] Even in relation to breach by the seller, the Act makes relatively little use of the concept of warranty. All the statutorily implied terms relating to correspondence with description,[13] to quality,[14] and to correspondence with sample,[15] as well as the principal implied term as to title,[16] are conditions; only the implied terms as to freedom

---

[4] *Kwei Tek Chao v British Traders Ltd* [1954] QB 459, 480.

[5] The general rule is usually traced back to Lord Mansfield's judgment in *Boone v Eyre* (1777) 1 Hy Bl 273 n, 2 W Bl 312; see Treitel, *The Law of Contract* (10th edn, 1999) 713–721.

[6] Ibid 721–751.   [7] S 61(1).   [8] S 11(3) and (4).

[9] eg *Bunge Corp of New York v Tradax Export SA* [1981] 1 WLR 711 (p 120 *post*).

[10] S 10(1).   [11] Ss 39(1)(c), 47, 48.

[12] S 48(4).   [13] S13(1) and (1A).   [14] S 14(2), (3), and (6).

[15] S 15(2) and (3).   [16] S 12(1) and (5A).

from encumbrances and as to quiet possession are warranties.[17] The concept of a 'condition' in the Sale of Goods Act sense is by no means restricted to contracts for the sale of goods: it applies to contracts generally: for example, to charterparties where statements as to the position of the ship[18] and as to the date of sailing[19] have been held to have the effect of conditions (though in the nineteenth century they were sometimes rather confusingly called warranties).[20]

Now we next have to ask why it is that the injured party should want to seek what I have called rescission, in response to the other's breach. One reason may be that it is a convenient remedy: a justified refusal to perform avoids the need to go to court. Another is that it is the most appropriate remedy: a buyer who buys goods for use may find that, on account of the non-conformity, they are useless for his intended purpose (or significantly less useful for that purpose than he had expected) and rejection in such a case makes good practical sense. But a third reason lies precisely in the fact that the purpose and effect of the remedies that I have grouped together under the name of rescission is to *undo* a contract: this makes them attractive to an injured party who wants to get out of the contract especially where his reason for wanting to do so has nothing to do with the breach, as in some of the situations to be discussed shortly. So long as the concept of a 'condition' was based on the notion that a condition was (to invert the Sale of Goods Act definition of warranty) a term *central* to the main purpose of the contract, it was reasonable to assume that any breach of condition would cause serious prejudice to the injured party and to hold that it should therefore entitle that party to rescind. No doubt this notion was, historically, one of the bases of the concept;[21] and it still appears in Diplock LJ's

---

[17] S 12(2), (4), (5), and (5A).
[18] *Behn v Burness* (1863) 3 B & S 751.
[19] *Glaholm v Hays* (1841) 2 M & G 257; cf *Bentsen v Taylor* [1893] 2 QB 274.
[20] eg in *Behn v Burness* (n 18 *supra*) 755.
[21] eg *Glaholm v Hays* (n 19 *supra*) 266 (performance of the term going 'to the very root of the contract').

definition of 'condition' in the *Hong Kong Fir* case. A condition, he there says, is 'an undertaking . . . of which it can be predicated that every breach . . . will deprive the party not in default of substantially the whole benefit which it was intended that he should obtain from the contract'.[22] But this was not the way in which the concept of condition developed. The legal classification of a term as a condition was applied (as Lord Roskill has said) to many 'terms the breaches of which do *not* deprive the innocent party of substantially the whole of the benefit which he was intended to receive from the contract'.[23] The reason for this development was that the concept of a 'condition' became stereotyped: once a particular *kind* of term—eg that as to correspondence of goods with the contractual description—had been classified by statute or by judicial decision as a condition,[24] then in future cases *any* breach of that term justified rescission, even though in a particular case the breach caused no serious (or any) prejudice to the injured party.

It is this possibility that leads to trouble. A party—it may be either buyer or seller, either recipient or provider of services—has some good commercial reason for wanting to rescind a contract, but that reason gives him no legal ground for doing so. He then discovers some other, possibly quite minor or commercially insignificant, nonconformity in the other's performance and relies on that as a ground for rescission. One well-known illustration is provided by *Re Moore and Landauer*[25] where a buyer of tinned Australian fruit wanted to reject the goods because there had been a considerable delay in their arrival in England. This was not a matter for which the seller was responsible and so not a ground for rejection. But the contract provided that the tins were to be packed in cases of

---

[22] *Hong Kong Fir Shipping Co Ltd v Kawasaki Kisen Kaisha Ltd* [1962] 2 QB 26, 69; see further at n 41, *infra*.

[23] *Bunge Corp of New York v Tradax Export SA* [1981] 1 WLR 711, 724.

[24] Sale of Goods Act 1979, s 13; for judicial classification of terms as conditions, see *ante* at nn 18 and 19.

[25] [1921] 2 KB 519.

thirty tins each and a substantial part of the consignment was packed in cases of twenty-four tins each. This discrepancy was held to justify rejection as it amounted to a breach of the implied condition that the goods must correspond with the contractual description. There was no evidence that the breach prejudiced the buyer: the court merely hypothesized that it might have done so.[26] Another common situation is that in which a party's real motive for rescinding is that the market has moved against him and he seizes on some possibly quite minor breach of a term which has been classified as a condition as an excuse for escaping from what has for him become a bad bargain. The point is well illustrated by *Arcos Ltd v Ronaasen*[27] where buyers of timber from a Russian government agency rejected it and refused to pay. Their motive for rejection, no doubt, was a fall in the market price, while their originally stated ground for rejection was that the timber was not a 'summer shipment' as required by the contract. Having failed to substantiate this point, they then made the (for them) lucky discovery that the timber was nine-sixteenths of an inch thick when the contract required it to be only half an inch thick. This discrepancy amounted to a breach of the implied condition as to correspondence with the contractual description. It therefore justified the buyers' rejection even though the extra thickness of the timber did not in the least affect its usefulness to them. In the Court of Appeal Scrutton LJ commented on this manoeuvre of the buyers with some acidity: 'I set off in my own mind, against that not very reasonable conduct of the buyers, the fact that I continually find the Russian Government, represented by its various agents, breaking its contracts with the most cheerful indifference to ordinary commercial principles. I therefore wipe out from my mind any prejudice on either side from what I see or know of either party.'[28]

Unfortunately, in spite of Scrutton LJ's animadversions,

Ibid 525 ('may be placed in considerable difficulty').

[1933] AC 470.

(1932) 37 Com Cas 291, 295.

this sort of conduct is by no means unusual in the reported cases. One common situation is that in which a commodity contract sets out a timetable for performance: for example, a contract made in April provides for goods to be shipped in October but they are shipped on 30 September or on 1 November. Nothing is more firmly settled in England than that, as a matter of common law, the stipulation as to the time of shipment is part of the contractual description of the goods, that the seller is therefore in breach of the implied condition as to correspondence with that description, and that the buyer can reject the goods[29] even though the fact of early or late shipment does not affect their value or prejudice the buyer in any other way and even though his motive for rejecting is that the market price of goods of the contract description has fallen between April and October. Conversely where it is the buyer who is in breach of a time stipulation the seller may be entitled to rescind (ie to refuse to deliver): eg where the buyer is to make shipping arrangements and to give notice of the ship's readiness to load but fails to give that notice within the time required by the contract.[30] It would make no difference that the delay did not prejudice the seller and that his motive for rescinding was that the market price for the goods had risen.

This state of the law gave rise to some dissatisfaction. In *Reardon Smith v Hansen Tangen* Lord Wilberforce said that cases on sales by description, such as *Re Moore and Landauer* were 'excessively technical and due for fresh examination in this House'[31]—though he excepted from his criticism 'sales of unascertained future goods (eg commodities) as to which each detail of the description must be assumed to be vital'.[32] So far, that 'fresh examination' has not taken place; perhaps because the courts have found another way of at least mitigating the excessive technicality.

---

[29] *Bowes v Shand* (1877) 2 App Cas 455.
[30] *Bunge Corp of New York v Tradax Export SA* (n 23 *supra*).
[31] [1976] 1 WLR 989, 998.
[32] Ibid. Presumably he regarded *Arcos Ltd v Ronaasen* (n 27 *supra*), to which he did not refer in the passage quoted in the text, as falling into this category.

2. INTERMEDIATE TERMS

The machinery used for this purpose was the invention, or perhaps more accurately the rediscovery, of a third type of contract term, now known as 'innominate' (because it has no name) or 'intermediate' (because it is thought to lie somewhere between conditions and warranties). The credit for this invention or discovery belongs to Diplock LJ, whose judgment in the *Hong Kong Fir* case[33] has a fair claim to being the most important judicial contribution to English contract law in the past century. Its importance was not immediately recognized, but twenty years later Lord Wilberforce was to describe it as a 'seminal judgment' which 'has since become classical';[34] and its influence has been enormous.

(a) The *Hong Kong Fir* Case

Let me begin with the facts of the *Hong Kong Fir* case. The ship (originally called *Antrim* but renamed *Hong Kong Fir*) was time chartered for twenty-four months in December 1956. At that time freight rates were very high in consequence of the closure of the Suez Canal during the first of a series of Suez crises. The amount payable by the charterers was '47s. per ton on the vessel's deadweight of 9,131 tons per 30 days'—or just under £15.5 million for the twenty-four month period. The ship was 'delivered' (ie made available for service under the charterparty) in February 1957, but she was unseaworthy and needed repairs, which took (on and off) twenty weeks, during which she was 'off hire', so that the charterers were relieved from their liability to pay to the extent of some £3 million. The repairs were not completed until September 1957, seven months after the original delivery. Meanwhile, the Suez Canal had been reopened and freight rates had fallen: in June 1957 to 24s. per ton and in mid-August to 13s. 6d. per ton, the latter

---

[33] [1962] 2 QB 26.
[34] *Bunge Corp of New York v Tradax Export SA* [1981] 1 WLR 711, 714, 715.

amount being between a quarter and a third of the rate fixed by the charterparty. In June, and again in September, the charterers purported to rescind the charterparty and they later tried to justify the rescission on two main grounds.

The first of these was that the delays in making the ship seaworthy were so serious as to 'frustrate' their purpose in entering into the charterparty. We do not actually know what that purpose was; we are not told whether they wanted to use the ship for their own (and if so for what) purposes, or whether they intended to 'sublet' her; in the latter event, the contract was simply one by which they had speculated on the freight market and lost. They certainly did not show that the delays in remedying the unseaworthiness had caused them any prejudice: on the contrary, one can argue that those delays *benefited* them to the extent of some £3 million in relieving them, for the twenty weeks that they lasted, from the obligation to pay the very high rate of hire reserved by the charter party. However all that may be, the Court rejected the argument that there had been a 'frustrating' breach; but the judgments do not make it at all clear exactly why the argument was rejected. Was it because twenty weeks formed only a small part of the twenty-four months? Or because, after the repairs had been carried out, there was no likelihood of further trouble with regard to seaworthiness? Or because the court suspected the charterers of using the unseaworthiness as a pretext for getting out of a bargain that other factors (ie the fall in the freight market) had turned, for the charterers, into a losing one? We simply cannot tell. The Court of Appeal give no reasons of their own for rejecting the argument that the breach had been a 'frustrating' one. They merely agree on this point with the judgment of Salmon J at first instance; and all that he says on the point is this: 'In the end, the problem is to look at the delay and the events which have occurred, against the period and other terms of the charterparty, and to decide whether in truth the circumstances in which performance is called for render it a thing radically different from that which was undertaken.' The answer to the question so put is given in just eight words: 'I reach the conclusion that they do not.'[35] Why? No reason is given and so we have to guess. I have (in this paragraph) made three guesses, but other possibilities cannot be excluded. It is of course precisely to avoid this kind of problem that the concept of a 'condition' (in the present sense) has evolved. Once a term has been classified as a condition, you do not have to ask the sort of question that Salmon J put to himself in the *Hong Kong Fir* case and you avoid the uncertainty which necessarily arises in attempting to answer questions of this kind.

So the second main argument put forward by the charterers tries to get away from the question put to himself by Salmon J: this second argument was that the term requiring the shipowner to provide a seaworthy ship was a 'condition' in the sense of a term, *any* breach of which justified rescission; on this basis, they claimed to be entitled to rescind *without* having to show that the unseaworthiness 'frustrated' their purpose or made the shipowners' performance (in the words of Salmon J) 'radically different from that which was undertaken'. But the Court of Appeal also rejected this argument and held that the term as to seaworthiness was not a 'condition' since it might be broken in some quite minor way (such as failure to provide a proper medical chest) and since rescission in respect of such a minor breach would be an inappropriate remedy—inappropriate, that is, in the sense of being unduly harsh to the party in breach[36] and not necessary for the protection of the injured party.[37] On the other hand, the term was not a 'warranty' either, at least in the Sale of Goods Act sense of a term for breach of which the sole remedy was by way of damages. In a passage that has become famous, Diplock LJ said: 'There are many contractual undertakings which

---

[35] [1962] 2 QB 26, 40.

[36] On the basis of the figures given above, rescission could have left the shipowners worse off by some £8.9 million if they had in consequence of it made a substitute contract in August 1957.

[37] There was no evidence that the unseaworthiness caused the charterers any loss.

cannot be categorised as being "conditions" or "warranties". Of such undertakings, all that can be predicated is that some breaches will and others will not, give rise to an event which will deprive the party not in default of substantially the whole benefit which it was intended that he should obtain.'[38] These are the terms now known as 'intermediate' or 'innominate'.[39] They differ from conditions in that a breach of them justifies rescission only if its effects are serious or 'frustrating' or led to a 'radical' difference between what was promised and what was performed. Exactly how they differ from warranties is less easy to explain; but one can with some confidence say that, in relation to them, there is no prima facie rule (as there is in relation to warranties)[40] that the remedy for breach is in damages and not by way of rescission.

Diplock LJ's judgment in the *Hong Kong Fir* case has been enormously influential, and I do not in any way want to detract from the extent of that influence or from its beneficial effect on the development of this branch of the law. But I must not gloss over the fact that it does give rise to a difficulty. This arises from Diplock LJ's definition in that case of a 'condition' as 'an undertaking . . . of which it can be predicated that every breach . . . will . . . deprive the party not in default of substantially the whole benefit which it was intended that he should obtain from the contract'.[41] That definition is the basis of his statement that the condition–warranty distinction is not exhaustive; but we have already seen that the definition is not entirely correct;[42] and indeed Lord Diplock himself drew back from it in the *Photo Production* case[43] where he refers to cases in which a breach by one party 'has the effect of depriving the other party of substantially the whole benefit which it was the intention of

---

[38] [1962] 2 QB 26, 70.

[39] *Bunge Corp of New York v Tradax Export SA* [1981] 1 WLR 711, 714.

[40] See the definition in Sale of Goods Act 1979, s 61(1), quoted at n 7 *ante.*

[41] [1962] 2 QB 26, 69 (*ante* at n 22).   [42] *Ante* at n 23.

[43] *Photo Production Ltd v Securicor Transport Ltd* [1980] AC 827, 847 referring to the *Hong Kong Fir* case.

the parties that he should obtain from the contract'.[44] This language is almost identical with that used by him in the *Hong Kong Fir* case to describe a breach of condition. But in the *Photo Production* case he describes this type of breach as a 'fundamental breach' and *contrasts* it with 'breach of condition' which (he says) arises 'where the parties have agreed, whether by express words or by implication of law that *any* failure by one party to perform a particular primary obligation . . . , irrespective of the gravity of the event that has in fact resulted from the breach, shall entitle the other party to elect to put an end to all primary obligations of both parties'.[45] This definition of 'condition' seems (if I may so put it) to blow the 'medical chest' example out of the water: you *can* have a term the breach of which may have either serious or trivial effects but which is nevertheless a condition. The point is now made even clearer by the Sale of Goods Act 1979, under the 1994 amendments to which the implied term as to satisfactory quality includes an undertaking that the goods are free from minor defects, and that implied term is a condition.[46] We shall see that a rather similar point can be made about time stipulations in a commercial context.[47]

It follows that the idea, presented in the *Hong Kong Fir* case, of an orderly hierarchy of terms is not quite accurate. We cannot say, as Diplock LJ there did, that terms are divided into

(*a*) conditions, *all* breaches of which cause serious prejudice,

(*b*) intermediate terms, *some* breaches of which cause serious prejudice, and

(*c*) warranties, *no* breaches of which cause serious prejudice.

The reason why we cannot say this is that 'conditions' so to speak straddle 'intermediate' terms because, although

---

[44] [1980] AC 827, 849.   [45] Ibid.

[46] S 14(2B)(c). 'Quality' in s 14(2B) refers back to s 14(2), so that the implied term referred to in the text above is a condition by virtue of s 14(6).

[47] See p 119 *post*.

some breaches of condition do cause serious prejudice, others justify rescission even though they do not cause serious prejudice or any prejudice at all. So the structure of Diplock LJ's judgment has to be reviewed in the light of later accounts (including his own) of the concept of 'condition'. But this theoretical point does not in any way affect the practical utility of the concept of the intermediate term.

(b) Development and Policies

That concept has acquired what may without too much exaggeration be called an enthusiastic following. An important development took place in 1975 when the Court of Appeal held in *The Hansa Nord*[48] that the concept applied to contracts for the sale of goods even though there was no recognition of it in the language or structure of the Sale of Goods Act. On the merits of *The Hansa Nord*, the case for applying the intermediate term concept was a strong one: the buyer was trying to reject the goods so as to secure for himself a saving of about £66,000 when the loss due to the seller's breach amounted to no more than £21,000 at the most. The Court of Appeal obviously viewed this manoeuvre with distaste and held that the buyer was not entitled to reject. 'Contracts' said Roskill LJ, 'are made to be performed and not to be avoided according to the whims of market fluctuation.'[49] In accordance with the same general policy, we find judicial statements to the effect that, in cases of first impression, the court should 'lean in favour'[50] of classifying previously unclassified terms as intermediate terms. That was, for example, the view of Slynn J in *Tradax v Goldschmidt*[51] where a contract for the sale of barley allowed for up to '4% foreign matters' and a certificate of quality stated the percentage of such matters to be 4.1 per cent. It was held that this was not a breach of condition but

---

[48] *Cehave NV v Bremer Handelsgesellschaft mbH (The Hansa Nord)* [1976] QB 44.
[49] [1976] QB 44, 71.
[50] eg *Tradax International SA v Goldschmidt* [1977] 2 Lloyd's Rep 604, 612; cf *Torvald Klaveness A/S v Arni Maritime Corp (The Gregos)* [1994] 1 WLR 1465, 1475.
[51] n 50 supra.

only one of an intermediate term, and that the breach was not sufficiently serious to give the buyer a right to reject. Such cases promote justice by preventing what may, without being too tendentious, be called abuses of the right to reject.

But there are also at least two countervailing policies which favour the classification of terms as conditions. The first relates to private consumers, who are much less well placed than most commercial buyers to deal with even quite minor non-conformity. That seems to be the policy behind the Sale of Goods Act provision, already mentioned, relating to minor defects.[52] The second policy applies in the commercial field where the courts have stressed the importance of promoting certainty. This policy again favours the classification of terms as conditions, in the sense that, once a term has been so classified, the victim of a breach of it in a future case will know as soon as he becomes aware of the breach that he can safely rescind without having to prove anything about the gravity of the breach.

The point is most clearly illustrated by cases of the kind, already mentioned, in which goods are shipped outside the shipment period specified in the contract: under the English common law,[53] the buyer can reject those goods if they are shipped by so much as a day or (I venture to say) an hour outside that period. That rule can now be explained as an application of the statutory classification of the term in question as a condition: the term specifying the shipment period is regarded as part of the description of the goods, so that shipment outside that period amounts to a breach of condition under section 13 of the Sale of Goods Act 1979. But the same policy consideration can also apply to a time stipulation which is not covered by any such statutory classification: for example, where it is the buyer who fails to perform such a stipulation. That is the significance of *Bunge*

---

[52] S 14(2B)(c) (n 46 *supra*).
[53] *Bowes v Shand* (1877) 2 App Cas 455. A different view has been taken in the United States: see *National Importing & Trading Co, Inc v EA Bear & Co* 155 NE 343 (1927), where *Bowes v Shand* was cited, but not followed, by the majority of the court.

Corp v Tradax Export[54] where the process of delivery was a collaborative enterprise: the seller was to choose the port at, and the buyer to provide the ship on, which the goods were to be loaded by the seller within a specified period and at a specified daily rate; and the buyer was to give at least fifteen days' notice to the seller of the ship's readiness to load. That notice arrived five days late and it was held that the term specifying the length of the notice was a condition so that the seller was entitled to rescind. The idea was to promote certainty: the seller could tell at once, on receipt of the notice, whether he was bound to deliver; he did not have to go into the question how much, if any, prejudice to him resulted from the fact that the notice was late.

There has been something of a flood of cases on the question whether other stipulations as to the time of performance are to be classified as conditions or as intermediate terms; and it has to be said that they present a somewhat confused picture, the details of which are beyond the scope of this lecture. Some cases stress the element of interdependence of the seller's and buyer's obligations which was a feature of *Bunge v Tradax*;[55] others do not regard this element as vital.[56] Some classify time clauses as conditions even where they are of no commercial importance;[57] others classify such time clauses as innominate terms.[58] Some classify the stipulation as a condition even though it specifies no *precise* time but provides merely for an act to be done 'as soon as possible';[59] others classify such terms as innominate since certainty cannot be promoted by classifying terms as conditions where they do not tell the parties exactly when

---

[54] *Bunge Corp of New York v Tradax Export SA* [1981] 1 WLR 711.

[55] *Supra.* cf *Gill & Duffus SA v Soc. Pour l'Exportation des Sucres SA* [1986] Lloyd's Rep 332; and see *Universal Bulk Carriers Ltd v Andre & Cie* [2001] 2 Lloyd's Rep 65, [2001] EWCA Civ 588, [28].

[56] eg *Greenwich Marine Inc v Federal Commerce & Navigation Co (The Mavro Vetranic)* [1985] 1 Lloyd's Rep 580, 585.

[57] *Michael J Warde v Feedex International Inc* [1985] 2 Lloyd's Rep 289, 298.

[58] *State Trading Corp of India v M Golodetz Ltd* [1981] 2 Lloyd's Rep 277.

[59] *Société Italo-Belge pour le Commerce et l'Industrie v Palm & Vegetable Oils (Malaysia) Sdn Bhd (The Post Chaser)* [1981] 2 Lloyd's Rep 695.

the act in question is to be done.[60] The difficulty of discerning an entirely coherent pattern in all these cases reflects the conflict between the two underlying policies: on the one hand, that of promoting certainty and, on the other, that of preventing what are perceived as abuses of the right to rescind. In relation to time clauses in commercial contracts, the first of these policies seems for two reasons to be in the ascendant. First, delay is an easy type of breach to establish, much easier than alleged qualitative breaches, in relation to which there can be many disputes of fact; and, secondly, delay is of obvious commercial importance where goods or services are dealt with on financial markets.

3. SALE OF GOODS ACT 1979, SECTION 15A

The common law on this subject is difficult enough; but now we have to fit into the scheme of the tripartite division of terms the new section 15A added, on the recommendation of the Law Commissions,[61] to the Sale of Goods Act in 1994;[62] similar provisions apply to other contracts for the supply of goods.[63] The new section applies only where the buyer is *not* a consumer; in such cases it restricts his right to reject the goods for breach of the statutorily implied terms as to correspondence with description or sample and as to quality. If the seller is guilty of such a breach but can show that the breach is 'so slight that it would be unreasonable' for the buyer to reject the goods, then the breach is 'not to be treated as a breach of condition but may be treated as a breach of warranty'. It follows that the buyer's remedy (if any) will be by way of damages only; and where the breach causes him no prejudice he will have no remedy at all. The policy underlying this provision is clearly to prevent the

---

[60] *Bremer Handelsgesellschaft mbH v Vanden Avenne-Izegem PVBA* [1978] 2 Lloyd's Rep 109 (so far as it relates to the notice under clause 21 of the contract).

[61] Report on *Sale and Supply of Goods*, Law Com No 160, Scot. Law Com No 104 (1987).

[62] See s 4(1) of the Sale and Supply of Goods Act 1994.

[63] Ibid, s 7(1).

(commercial) buyer from rejecting on grounds which are thought to be without merit; its aim is (in the words of the Law Commissions) to 'prevent rejection in bad faith'[64] though in this respect the section is curiously lopsided: it operates only against buyers and does not restrict the right of a seller to rescind (as for example in *Bunge v Tradax Export*).[65] Where it does apply, has it turned breaches of condition into breaches of intermediate terms? I think not, since it leaves intact the right to rescind where the breach is not 'slight'; and a breach which is not 'slight' may nevertheless not be so serious as to justify rescission for breach of an intermediate term.

My greatest concern with section 15A is whether it has any effect on the well-settled rule that the shipment of goods outside the contractually specified shipment period justifies rejection.[66] If it does qualify this rule, then it has destroyed the certainty which the rule is intended to promote. The Law Commissions' Report which led to the passing of the section seems to envisage that it is not to apply in such cases,[67] but the section itself contains no provision to that effect. It merely says that it will not apply where 'a contrary intention appears in, or is to be implied from, the contract'. Certainty can of course be restored by an express provision excluding the section, and, as such a provision is permitted by the section, it is presumably unlikely that it would be held unreasonable under the Unfair Contract Terms Act 1977. But in the absence of such an express provision, who can tell with certainty when one will be implied? The Law Commissions seek to allay these fears by saying that the section is 'not intended as a major alteration of the law'[68] and that the resulting 'uncertainty will be more apparent than real'[69]—a statement which is not explained but may be based on the idea that the section will not often apply, or that 'in the appropriate circumstances' it 'will not be difficult to infer . . . an intention'[70] to

<hr>

[64] (n 61 *supra*) §4.18. [65] n 54 *supra*.
[66] *Bowes v Shand* (1877) 2 App Cas 455 (*ante* at n 53).
[67] §4.24. [68] §4.2.
[69] §4.23. [70] Ibid.

exclude the section. But I am, with respect, not convinced and my scepticism derives, I think, some support from remarks made by Lord Hoffmann in the analogous context of a buyer's failure to perform a stipulation as to time in a contract for the sale of land where the stipulation is of the essence. In the *Union Eagle*[71] case the buyer was a mere ten minutes late in tendering payment. The contract provided for forfeiture of his deposit in the event of the buyer's failure to tender full payment on time; and his claim for relief against such forfeiture was rejected. To subject the forfeiture term to a judicial discretion to grant relief would (it was said) subvert certainty even if it was unlikely that the discretion would be exercised: 'its mere existence enables litigation to be employed as a negotiating tactic'.[72] Section 15A is capable of leading to exactly such a result; and the question is not *how often* it will be applied: uncertainty results from the fact that the buyer (or his legal adviser) cannot tell *when* it will be applied. My only consolation is that, so far as I know, the section has not been applied in any reported case.

4. INTERMEDIATE TERMS AND WARRANTIES

I have said[73] that section 15A does not turn conditions into intermediate terms because to exclude the right to reject where the breach is 'so slight' that rejection would be unreasonable is not the same thing as to restrict the right to cases in which the breach is so serious as (in Diplock LJ's words) to deprive the buyer of substantially the whole benefit which it was intended that he should obtain. There is also the converse question whether the concept of the intermediate term has swallowed up that of warranty. In his judgment in the *Hong Kong Fir* case, Diplock LJ describes a warranty as a contractual undertaking 'of which it can be predicated that *no* breach can give rise to an event

---

[71] *Union Eagle Ltd v Golden Achievement Ltd* [1997] AC 514.

[72] Ibid 519.

[73] *Supra*, after n 65.

which will deprive the party not in default of substantially the whole benefit which it was intended that he should obtain from the contract'[74]—and where the term is of this kind, then the injured party will not be entitled to rescind. That is also the assumption underlying the definition of warranty in section 61(1) of the Sale of Goods Act where it is said that the breach of a warranty 'gives rise to a claim for damages, but *not* to a right to reject the goods and treat the contract as repudiated'. Nevertheless, there is the possibility that the breach of a term which is a warranty because it is (within the words of that definition) 'collateral to the main purpose of the contract' may, in exceptional circumstances, have unexpectedly serious effects; and there is some support in the judgment of Ormrod LJ in *The Hansa Nord* for the view that, if a seller's breach of warranty does have such effects, or if the breach is one which is deliberate in the sense that the seller could easily put it right but refuses to do so, then the buyer could reject.[75] It is quite hard to think of a realistic sale of goods example since the ambit of the statutorily implied terms as to quality or fitness for a particular purpose is now[76] so wide and since all these terms are classified by the Sale of Goods Act as conditions. Perhaps we might take the case of a contract for the hire of a car in which the owner 'warranted' to make the car available at 8 am on Derby Day and then the previous day told the hirer that it would not be available until 8 pm. In all probability, the court would conclude that the word 'warranty' was not here used in its technical sense but meant 'condition'. But if for some reason the drafting precluded this line of reasoning, the court might well hold that in such a case it was not appropriate to require the hirer to pay the agreed hire and then to claim damages; and that the breach, though one of 'warranty', justified his immediate cancellation of the contract.

In the case of a contract for the sale of goods, it could

---

[74] [1962] 2 QB 26, 70.　　　　　　　　[75] [1976] QB 44, 83.

[76] ie after the amendment of the Sale of Goods Act 1979 (especially of s 14) by the Sale and Supply of Goods Act 1994.

similarly be argued that, just as the statutory condition–warranty distinction is not exhaustive and leaves room under the rules of common law (saved by section 62(2)) for the concept of the intermediate term, so the Sale of Goods Act does not exhaustively state the *effects* of the distinction. Ormrod LJ's suggestion has not so far been tested, presumably because breach of warranty is, by reason of the statutory definition of 'warranty', quite unlikely to have an effect sufficiently serious to justify rescission. It should also be recalled that statutory classification of terms as 'warranties' is rare (and confined to cases where damages are an entirely appropriate remedy). Where the term is *not* classified as a warranty either by legislation or by the express agreement of the parties, it would be more than somewhat eccentric for a court to classify it as such and then to say that the effect of its breach was so serious as to justify rejection or rescission. The court would be much more likely to take the obvious route of classifying the term as intermediate and then saying that rescission was justified on account of the seriousness breach.

Even if Ormrod LJ's suggestion were accepted (so that in exceptional cases breach of warranty were a ground of rescission), the concept of warranty would still be distinct from that of the intermediate term. To put the matter at its lowest, the definition of 'warranty' in the Sale of Goods Act 1979 lays down a prima facie rule that breach of warranty does not give rise to a right to rescind, while in the case of the breach of an intermediate term there is no prima facie rule either way. The view that intermediate terms have not swallowed up warranties is also supported by many judicial discussions which divide the types of terms so far considered into *three* classes: ie conditions, intermediate terms, and warranties. [77]

There is one last difficulty in this context: this is that some judges have continued the nineteenth century

---

[77] eg *Bunge Corp of New York v Tradax Export SA* [1981] 1 WLR 711, 725; *Photo Production Ltd v Securicor Transport Ltd* [1980] AC 827, 849 (general rule subject to two exceptions: this amounts to a threefold classification).

practice[78] of calling terms 'warranties' when (in the now current terminology) they are really 'conditions'. The nineteenth century usage is well illustrated by *Behn v Burness* where the term under discussion was a statement in a charterparty as to the position of the ship, and this term was said to be 'a warranty, that is to say a condition'.[79] As late as 1982 Lord Diplock throughout his speech in *Lambert v Lewis*[80] referred to one of the terms classified as a *condition* by the Sale of Goods Act[81] as a warranty. The same terminology has been used in relation to the term implied at common law that goods which are bought in circumstances involving transit before use are, when shipped, in such a state that they can endure normal transit. This term is described in the cases as an implied 'warranty';[82] but the context (especially the use in this connection of the word 'merchantable'[83] which was formerly[84] the basis of an implied condition under the Sale of Goods Act) clearly shows that 'warranty' is here used, not in its current Sale of Goods Act sense, but to refer to a term in the nature of a condition (in the language of the 1979 Act). Breach of the implied term here under discussion no doubt justifies rescission, but this conclusion lends no support to the view that this remedy is available for breach of a 'warranty' properly so called in the Sale of Goods Act sense.

5. INSURANCE WARRANTIES

The use of the expression 'warranty' to mean 'condition' has also survived in insurance law. Section 33(3) of the Marine Insurance Act 1906 provides that 'A warranty . . . is a condition which must be exactly complied with'—

---

[78] *Ante* at n 20.   [79] (1863) 3 B & S 751, 755.

[80] [1982] AC 225, 273, 276.   [81] S 14.

[82] *Mash & Murrell Ltd v Joseph I Emanuel Ltd* [1961] 1 WLR 862, 865; (for the ultimate decision in this case, see [1961] 2 Lloyd's Rep 326); *AB Kemp Ltd v Tolland* [1956] 1 Lloyd's Rep 681, 685.

[83] In the *Mash & Murrell* case (*supra*) [1961] 1 WLR 862, 865.

[84] Sale of Goods Act 1979, s 14(2), before its amendment by Sale and Supply of Goods Act 1994.

language curiously reminiscent of the phrase from *Behn v Burness* just quoted.[85] The subsection goes on: 'If it be not so complied with, then, subject to any express provision in the policy, the insurer is discharged from liability as from the date of the breach of warranty.' So in one important respect such a 'warranty' resembles a 'condition' in the Sale of Goods Act and in the general law: failure to comply with it relieves the insurer from liability. But, as explained by Lord Goff in *The Good Luck*,[86] the effect of breach of an insurance 'warranty'—eg of breach by an insured shipowner of his promise not to take his ship into a 'prohibited area'—differs from breach of a Sale of Goods Act 'condition' in that breach of an insurance 'warranty' automatically discharges the insurer while breach of a Sale of Goods Act (or other) 'condition' discharges the buyer (or other injured party) only if he so elects: under the 1906 Act the insurer 'is discharged'[87] by the breach while under the 1979 Act the breach 'may give rise to a right to treat the contract as repudiated'.[88] The reason for this difference lies not, I think, in any difference between the nature of an insurance 'warranty' and a Sale of Goods Act 'condition', but in the nature of a contract of indemnity insurance, ie one by which the insurer promises to indemnify the insured against loss. Under such a contract the insured does not pay for a *performance* (as a buyer or shipper of goods does); he pays, or bargains, for a conditional *promise* which in the great majority of cases does not have to be performed at all because the event insured against normally does not happen. Before the breach of warranty, the insurer is bound by his conditional promise (or is 'on risk') but not of course liable to make any payment if no loss occurs. After the breach of warranty, he is no longer bound by his conditional promise: this seems to be what the Act means by saying he is 'discharged'. If 'discharge' required election, the insurer would find

---

[85] At n 79, *ante*.
[86] *Bank of Nova Scotia v Hellenic Mutual War Risk Association (Bermuda) Ltd (The Good Luck)* [1992] 1 AC 233.
[87] Marine Insurance Act 1906, s 33(3).
[88] Sale of Goods Act 1979, s 11(3).

himself in considerable difficulty as he usually would not
know of the breach of warranty until after the loss had
occurred. Much the simplest solution of this difficulty is the
one provided by the Act—ie discharge of the insurer as
from the date of the breach. For this practical reason, the
insurance 'warranty' and the 'condition' in other contracts
operate in slightly different ways, but I do not think that
they belong to distinct legal categories. So at this stage we
are still left with three of my initial four types of terms.

6. FUNDAMENTAL TERMS

(a) Exemption Clauses and Fundamental Breach

My fourth type of term is the so-called 'fundamental term'.
This was part of the armoury developed by the courts in
their efforts to restrict the operation of exemption clauses
before legislation either invalidated such clauses or gave
the courts wide powers to invalidate them on grounds of
unreasonableness or unfairness. As is well known, the
courts to this end developed the doctrine of 'fundamental
breach', and at one time this doctrine was considered as a
matter of substantive law to prevent a party from excluding
or limiting liability for certain very serious breaches. But in
1966 the House of Lords in the *Suisse Atlantique* case[89] drew
back from this 'substantive doctrine' and declared the rule
to be one of construction only, though it took three further
decisions of the House, the *Photo Production*[90] case in 1980,
and the *George Mitchell*,[91] and *Ailsa Craig*[92] cases in 1983, to
establish the point with anything approaching decisive-
ness. We are left with a rule of construction by which
general words in exemption clauses will not cover certain
very serious breaches: to cover such a breach the clause

---

[89] *Suisse Atlantique Société d'Armement Maritime SA v NV Rotterdamsche Kolen
Centrale* [1967] 1 AC 361.
[90] *Photo Production Ltd v Securicor Transport Ltd* [1980] AC 827.
[91] *George Mitchell (Chesterhall) Ltd v Finney Lock Seeds Ltd* [1983] 2 AC 803.
[92] *Ailsa Craig Fishing Co Ltd v Malvern Fishing Co Ltd* [1983] 1 WLR 964.

must be 'most clearly and unambiguously expressed'.[93] Even after the four cases to which I have referred, we still occasionally find courts deciding cases of this kind on the basis that a literal interpretation of the clause cannot possibly have accorded with 'the true common intention of the parties';[94] and such decisions have much the same effect as the old 'substantive doctrine' of fundamental breach even though the judgments in them generally make a bow in the direction of the 'construction' principle.

Driven into a corner by the 'construction' theory initiated in 1966, the Court of Appeal in 1970 tried in effect to reintroduce a version of the substantive doctrine through an ingenious back door. The argument was that the fundamental breach gave the injured party a right to rescind the contract and that, on his exercise of that right, he brought the whole contract to an end with the result that he was no longer bound by the exemption clause even though, on its true construction, it excluded or restricted his right to damages for the breach. That was the reasoning of the *Harbutt's Plasticine* case;[95] but (as again is well known) it was rejected by the House of Lords in the *Photo Production* case[96] in 1980. The injured party's rescission put an end to obligations of *further* performance which would, but for the election to rescind, have accrued after the time of the rescission; but it did not operate retrospectively so that loss which had occurred *before* the rescission continued to be governed by the clause.

(b) Concept of Fundamental Term

The concept of a fundamental *term* plays only a subsidiary, but nevertheless a significant and doctrinally interesting, part in this familiar story. There were, and are, many ways

---

[93] Ibid 966.

[94] eg *Tor Line AB v Alltrans Group of Canada Ltd (The TFL Prosperity)* [1984] 1 WLR 48, 59; *Wibau Maschinenfabrik Hartman SA v Mackinnon & Co (The Chanda)* [1989] 2 Lloyd's Rep 494.

[95] *Harbutt's 'Plasticine' Ltd v Wayne Tank & Pump Co Ltd* [1970] 1 QB 447.

[96] n 90 *supra*.

of committing a breach which used to attract the operation of the substantive doctrine and which now attract the operation of the rule of construction; and one kind of breach which has this effect is the breach of a fundamental term. Such a term is one the breach of which makes the performance rendered not merely defective but essentially different from that promised: the classic case of a breach of a fundamental term is that of a seller who delivers peas when he had contracted to deliver beans.[97] Such a term is, in the words of Devlin J, 'narrower than a condition of the contract'.[98] To use his examples, a seller of 'mahogany logs' would be in breach of a fundamental term if he delivered pine logs while a seller of 'mahogany logs equal to sample' would be in breach of condition if he delivered mahogany logs not up to sample.[99] The distinction is not, of course, always as clear as this since a fundamental term can be broken even though the thing is not literally a different thing from that promised, but is so seriously defective as to be different in substance. In the *George Mitchell* case[100] there were (at various stages) considerable differences of judicial opinion on the point,[101] the answer to which turns, in the last resort, on the construction of the contract. A seed merchant had supplied seed to a farmer which grew into vegetation fit for neither human nor animal consumption; photographs of the crop were taken which showed the seller's representative 'looking about as worried as it is possible for an individual to look'.[102] Parker J[103] and a majority of the Court of Appeal held that 'what was delivered was simply not fulfilment of the contract, not even defective performance any more than delivery of a motor bicycle would be fulfilment of a contract for the sale of a

---

[97] See *Chanter v Hopkins* (1838) 4 M & W 399, 404.

[98] *Smeaton Hanscomb & Co Ltd v Sassoon I Setty, Son & Co (No 1)* [1953] 1 WLR 1468, 1470.

[99] Ibid.   [100] n 91 *supra*.

[101] Contrast the views of Parker J [1981] 1 Lloyd's Rep 476, 480 and that of the majority of the Court of Appeal [1983] 2 QB 284, 385 with that which prevailed in the House of Lords [1983] 2 AC 803, 813 (*infra* at n 105).

[102] [1981] 1 Lloyd's Rep 476, 477–78.   [103] Ibid 480.

car'.[104] But the House of Lords disagreed, Lord Bridge saying that 'this is not a "peas and beans" case at all'.[105] Fortunately for the farmer, this did not affect the outcome since the supplier's exemption clause failed to comply with the statutory requirement of reasonableness then in force.

Does any of this matter now that the substantive doctrine has been rejected in favour of a rule of construction? I am afraid that it does for a number of reasons.

(c) Problems of Construction

First, under the rule of construction we do still have to ask whether the words of the exemption clause are wide enough to cover the breach of a fundamental term. The point may be illustrated by *Aron v Comptoir Wegimont*,[106] decided by McCardie J in 1921, long before the growth of all the learning about fundamental breach and fundamental term. There a contract for the sale of cocoa powder stated (in effect) that the consignment had been shipped in October when actually it was shipped in November. The contract contained a non-rejection clause which applied 'whatever the difference of the shipment may be in value from the grade, type *or description* specified'. This was held not to prevent the buyer from rejecting since the express requirement that the goods were to be shipped in October was 'a good deal more than mere description of the goods'[107] so as to put the seller in breach of condition under section 13 of the Sale of Goods Act. The reasoning of the case is not at all easy to follow, but a possible modern rationalization of it would be that the seller was in breach of a fundamental term and that the words of the non-rejection clause did not on their true construction cover that breach. The rule of construction may leave it open to the draftsman to cover even such a breach; but there are in practice likely to be a number of constraints on his freedom of action. One

---

[104] [1983] 2 QB 284, 305.   [105] [1983] 2 AC 803, 813.
[106] *J Aron & Co v Comptoir Wegimont* [1921] 3 KB 435.
[107] Ibid 440.

132 *Types of Contractual Terms*

is that an exemption clause, if contained in the supplier's 'written standard terms of business',[108] may be subject to the requirement of reasonableness under the Unfair Contract Terms Act 1977 (though this would not apply to international supply contracts, such as that in the *Aron* case). The well-known example of a deliberate breach leading to loss or destruction of the subject matter comes to mind: an exemption clause purporting in terms to cover a breach of this kind could well be held not to satisfy the requirement of reasonableness. Another constraint on the draftsman is the common law rule that the court may refuse to give effect to words which are literally wide enough to cover the breach because (in the words of Lord Reid in the *Suisse Atlantique* case) to do so would 'lead to an absurdity'.[109] This common law principle could apply where the breach was deliberate in the sense just given. It may also be illustrated by *The TFL Prosperity*,[110] a charterparty case in which the shipowner's breach consisted of supplying a ship which was not of the specified dimensions and the House of Lords refused to give literal effect to words excluding his liability for this breach since the result of doing so would be that 'the charter virtually ceases to be a contract ... and becomes no more than a statement of intent by the owner'.[111] Faced with these legislative and common law constraints, the draftsman may well be driven to frame his exemption clauses in words that still leave considerable scope for the operation of the concept of a fundamental term.

(d) Deviation

The second reason why that concept retains, or may retain, some degree of practical importance lies in the fact that there is no doubt that one legal consequence of breach of a fundamental term, like that of breach of condition, is to give

---

[108] Unfair Contract Terms Act 1977, s 3(1).
[109] *Suisse Atlantique* case (n 89 *supra*) [1967] 1 AC 361, 398.
[110] (n 94 *supra*) [1984] 1 WLR 48.
[111] Ibid 58–59.

the injured party the right to rescind the contract. The general rule is that such rescission does not operate retro-spectively in the sense that it does not deprive the guilty party of the protection of an exemption clause in respect of loss suffered before the time of the election to rescind: that is the outcome of the *Photo Production* case.[112] But there is a well-known exception to this position in the law relating to contracts for the carriage of goods by sea (and in a number of analogous situations).[113] In such contracts, the term as to the route to be taken is regarded as fundamental;[114] any unjustified departure from that route amounts to a breach known as a deviation; any deviation justifies rescission by the cargo-owner even though the deviation is only slight and 'for practical purposes irrelevant';[115] and deviation also deprives the carrier of the protection of (*inter alia*) exemp-tion and limitation clauses.[116] Deviation has this last effect even though the exemption or limitation clause covers the loss which has occurred and moreover it does so with retro-spective effect: that is, not merely from the time at which the shipper or charterer rescinds (if he ever does this) or from the time at which the loss or damage has occurred, but from the time of the deviation.[117] In these respects, the devi-ation cases appear not to apply the general rules laid down in the *Photo Production* case, where their authority is recog-nized[118] and they are described by Lord Wilberforce as *sui generis*.[119] Why should they, in this context, be so treated? The answer traditionally given to this question (an answer which may now have a new lease of life)[120] is that this is consistent with their rationale. This has been said to be that,

---

[112] (n 96 *supra*) [1980] AC 827.

[113] eg land carriage: *L & NW Ry V Neilson* [1922] 2 AC 263.

[114] See the reference to deviation in the *Smeaton Hanscomb* case (n 98 *supra*) [1953] 1 WLR 1468, 1470.

[115] *Suisse Atlantique* case (n 89 *supra*) [1967] 1 AC 361, 423. Cf *ante* at n 23 for a similar characteristic of breach of condition.

[116] See eg *Joseph Thorley Ltd v Orchis SS Co Ltd* [1907] 1 KB 660; *Hain SS Co v Tate & Lyle Ltd* (1936) 41 Com Cas 350.

[117] *Joseph Thorley* case (n 116 *supra*).   [118] [1980] AC 827, 845.

[119] Ibid 850.

[120] Because of *The Good Luck* (n 86 *supra*) [1992] 1 AC 233.

as a result of the deviation, the cargo-owner loses the benefit of his insurance cover and so ought to have remedies
against the carrier coextensive with those against the
underwriter which he has lost by reason of the carrier's
breach.[121] That reasoning is not entirely convincing because
the insurance contract may contain a 'held covered' clause;
but such a clause may also come with a sting in its tail: it
may provide that the insured is to be 'held covered in the
event of deviation *at a premium to be arranged*'; and insurers
have been known to 'arrange' the premium at the amount
of the loss.[122] So there may still be force in the 'insurance'
explanation of the deviation cases; and if there is, then we
have to ask just when deviation begins to relieve the insurer
from liability. The answer given to this question by section
46(1) of the Marine Insurance Act 1906 is that 'the insurer is
discharged from liability *as from the time of deviation*, and it
is immaterial that the ship may have regained her route
before the loss occurs'. Part of this wording closely resembles that of section 33(3) which provides that, in case of
breach of (an insurance) warranty 'the insurer is discharged
from liability *as from the date of the breach of warranty*'. We
now have the authority of *The Good Luck*[123] for saying that,
in breach of warranty cases, the insurer's discharge is auto-
matic, that is, it occurs without election on his part. On the
wording of the Act, it is hard to resist the conclusion that
the same is true in cases of deviation; and if the 'insurance'
explanation of the effect of deviation between cargo-owner
and carrier is accepted, then the same reasoning may, in the
light of *The Good Luck*, explain the retrospective effect of
deviation on exemption clauses.[124]

---

[121] *Hain SS Co* case (n 116 *supra*) (1936) 41 Com Cas 350, 354.

[122] *Vincentelli v Rowlett* (1911) 16 Com Cas 310; the question whether such a premium would be 'reasonable' within Marine Insurance Act 1906, s 31(2), awaits judicial determination.

[123] (n 86 *supra*) [1992] 1 AC 233.

[124] This argument at first sight is open to the objection that, under the Marine Insurance Act 1906, s 39, there is also an implied 'warranty' of seaworthiness, breach of which has the effect stated in s 33(3), as interpreted in *The Good Luck*, n 86 *supra*. Yet in contracts for the carriage of goods by sea and in time charters the term relating to seaworthiness is not even a 'condition', let alone a fundamental

I know that there are other explanations of the deviation cases: for example that Lord Diplock in the *Photo Production*[125] case called deviation a breach of condition. But Devlin J had earlier called it a breach of a fundamental term;[126] and where two such giants of commercial law as Lords Diplock and Devlin differ on such a point of classification, a retired law professor should perhaps not rush in, but I shall nevertheless declare myself to be a respectful adherent of Lord Devlin's view. Deviation may in one respect resemble breach of condition, ie in that it gives rise to a right to rescind even though it is 'for practical purposes irrelevant'[127] and this resemblance may account for Lord Diplock's classification of deviation as a breach of condition. But there are also clear legal differences (described above) between other legal effects of the two kinds of breach, particularly in relation to their respective effects on exemption clauses.[128] These also make it hard to support the view that the deviation cases should be 'assimilated into

term; it is no more than an innominate term, as was held in the *Hong Kong Fir* case (n 22 *supra*) [1962] 2 QB 26. For the purpose of determining the carrier's ability to rely on exclusions or limitations of liability provided by the contract of carriage, however, seaworthiness is regarded as an 'overriding obligation' so that if this obligation is not fulfilled 'and the non-fulfilment causes the damage' the carrier cannot rely on contractual immunities: *Maxine Footwear Co Ltd v Canadian Government Merchant Marine Co Ltd* [1959] AC 589, 609. This statement refers to 'immunities' provided by the Hague Rules, but the same principle applies at common law to immunities provided by a privately negotiated contract: see *Carver on Bills of Lading* (1st edn, 2001) §9–208. The effect of all this is in this respect similar to that of deviation that, if the cargo-owner suffers loss in consequence of unseaworthiness (and is deprived by reason of the breach of an insurance warranty of his rights against the underwriter), he will not be precluded by exemptions or limitations in the contract of carriage from asserting rights against the carrier. In this sense, unseaworthiness (like deviation) operates retrospectively and without any need (or indeed any right) on the part of the cargo-owner to rescind the contract of carriage. The two kinds of breach differ, however, in that the principle stated in the *Maxine Footwear* case applies only where the loss is *caused* by unseaworthiness; while in cases of deviation *Joseph Thorley Ltd v Orchis SS Co Ltd* [1907] 1 KB 667 holds that there is no need for any such causal link; for criticism of the latter case, see *Carver on Bills of Lading* (*supra*) §§9–059 *et seq*.

[125] (n 90 *supra*) [1980] AC 827, 850.
[126] In the *Smeaton Hanscomb* case (n 105 *supra*) [1953] 1 WLR 1468, 1470.
[127] *Supra* at n 115.
[128] *Ante* at n 117.

the general law of contract'.[129] On this view, the retrospective effect of deviation on exemption clauses would be derived from their construction; but this would require the sort of strained construction that is now deprecated in this branch of the law.[130] So my preference is for Lord Wilberforce's *'sui generis'* view,[131] and my conclusion is that the concept of breach of condition has not swallowed up that of breach of a fundamental term.

(e) Loss of Right to Rescind

That conclusion is also supported by another rule, which has nothing to do with exemption clauses. In certain circumstances the right to rescind a contract for breach may be lost by the subsequent conduct of the injured party: for example 'acceptance' of goods by a buyer bars his right to reject for breach of condition.[132] The question whether the buyer has 'accepted' the goods depends in part on whether he had had a reasonable opportunity of examining them;[133] and if he had had such an opportunity, then he may have accepted them even though he has not actually examined them or discovered the breach of condition. But although there is no clear authority precisely in point, I submit that all this would not apply where there had been a breach of a particularly serious kind, as in a 'peas for beans' case.[134] Of

---

[129] *Kenya Railways v Antares Co Pty Ltd (The Antares)* [1987] 1 Lloyd's Rep 424, 430.

[130] *George Mitchell* case (n 91 *supra*) [1983] 2 AC 803, 814; *Photo Production* case, (n 90 *supra*) [1980] AC 827, 851.

[131] Ibid 845; this view is further supported by another special effect of deviation: viz that it has been held to deprive the carrier of the benefit of exemption clauses even in respect of loss not caused by the deviation: see n 124 *supra*.

[132] Sale of Goods Act 1979, s 11(4).

[133] Ibid s 35(2), (4), and (5).

[134] Cf *Rowland v Divall* [1923] 2 KB 500, where the breach was one of the implied 'condition' as to the seller's title under Sale of Goods Act 1979, s 12(1), but must also have been regarded as fundamental as it was held to have given rise to a total failure of consideration and so to entitle the buyer to the return of the price even though he had done acts which would no doubt have amounted to 'acceptance' of the car if the seller had been in breach merely of one of the implied terms as to quality.

course if the buyer *knows* that peas have been delivered under a contract to sell beans, and decides to keep the peas, then it may be possible to infer a new contract to buy peas.[135] But if he has merely had the opportunity of discovering the truth and has not discovered it (eg if he has not opened bags containing peas but reasonably believed to contain beans), then no such inference can be drawn. Nevertheless, the mere fact that his conduct was such as would have amounted to acceptance of non-conforming beans should not deprive him of the right to reject, if peas have in fact been delivered. This is by no means the only example that could be given of the application of the concept of breach of a fundamental term concept in the context of rights to rescind;[136] but it suffices to reinforce the case for saying that the concept retains a separate existence and a considerable degree of practical importance.

My conclusion is that the claim with which this lecture began is made good so that, at the end of the twentieth century, there were (and indeed still are) four types of contractual terms.

---

[135] *Charterhouse Credit Co Ltd v Tolly* [1963] 2 QB 683, 710.

[136] For another possible example, see *Gill & Duffus SA v Berger & Co Inc* [1984] AC 382, 390 (c.i.f. buyer's duty to pay against conforming documents may not extend to the case in which the non-conformity of the goods falls into the 'peas for beans' category).

Index

conditions 110–11
effect 107–8
general rule 108
Roman law
agreements to vary contracts 11

terms of contract
conditions 107–12 *see also*
conditions
fundamental terms
concept 129–31
construction 131–2
deviation 132–6
exemption clauses 128–9
loss of right to rescind 136–7
innominate terms *see* intermediate
terms
intermediate terms 113–21 *see also*
intermediate terms
Sale of Goods Act 1979, s 15A
121–3
warranties 107–12 *see also*
warranties
third-party beneficiaries 5
trusts
privity 50–3
Tweddle v Atkinson, rule in 47
types of contractual terms 107–37
conditions 107–12 *see also* conditions
fundamental terms
concept 129–31
construction 131–32
deviation 132–6
exemption clauses 128–9
loss of right to rescind
136–7
generally 4

innominate terms *see* intermediate
terms
intermediate terms 113–21 *see also*
intermediate terms
Sale of Goods Act 1979, s 15A
121–3
warranties 107–12 *see also*
warranties

Uniform Commercial Code 3
United States
American Law Institute's Restate-
ment of Contracts 2–3
Field Code States 8
privity 47–8
Uniform Commercial Code 3

variation of contract
agreements *see* agreements to vary
contracts
vicarious immunity
exemption clauses 53–8
privity 53–8

warranties 107–12
conditions distinguished from
107–8
definition 108–9
insurance 126–8
intermediate terms and 123–6
rescission 109
Williams v Roffey Bros 18–23, 43–6
decreasing pacts and 43–6
earlier cases, relation to 20–3
facts 18–19
generally 18
results 18–19

Printed in the United Kingdom
by Lightning Source UK Ltd.
129913UK00001B/154/A